Healing After the Suicide

Of a

Loved One

Ann Smolin, C.S.W.,
and John Guinan, Ph.D.

A FIRESIDE BOOK
Published by Simon & Schuster

New York   London   Toronto   Sydney   Tokyo   Singapore

FIRESIDE
Simon & Schuster Building
Rockefeller Center
1230 Avenue of the Americas
New York, New York 10020

FIRESIDE and colophon are registered trademarks
of Simon & Schuster Inc.

Designed by Richard Oriolo
Manufactured in the United States of America

10 9 8 7 6 5 4 3 2 1

Library of Congress Cataloging-in-Publication Data is available

ISBN 0-671-79660-7

While the examples in this book are based on real people and their experiences, the authors have created composite characters and altered any characteristics that might identify individual clients. The ideas and suggestions in this book are intended to supplement, not replace, the medical advice of trained professionals. In addition, all matters regarding your health require medical supervision. Consult your physician before adopting the suggestions in this book, as well as about any condition that may require diagnosis or medical attention.

The authors and publishers disclaim any liability arising directly or indirectly from the use of this book.

We dedicate this book to all of the courageous men, women, and children who have been "the other victims of suicide" and who have shared their painful journeys with us. They have taught us that by sharing their struggles and growth with others they heal themselves. This book contains their stories.

Acknowledgments

The authors are both grateful to Martin Smolin, Ann's husband, who untiringly revised their writing, and to Gail Winston, their editor at Simon & Schuster, who edited whatever Martin may have missed.

We also thank Madeleine Morel, of 2M Communications, who first encouraged us to write about our experiences with survivors. Without her guidance into the world of writing and publishing this book might never have been written.

Ann Smolin would like to express her gratitude to all those at Westchester Jewish Community Services who recognized the need for suicide survivor services and have made them available for many years. Particular thanks go to Ronald Gaudia, executive director, and Alan Trager, associate executive director, for their continuing support of this work. Special acknowledgment is due to Barbara Pinto, CSW, who did the pioneering work with the WJCS group known as Families and Friends of Victims of Suicide, establishing it and setting it on its present course. Thanks also to Dr. Jeffrey Sacks, who while serving as a psychiatric consultant to the group during its formative years, gave invaluable support for the importance of its existence and clinical guidance in the treatment of survivors of suicide.

John Tiebout, who graciously and generously volunteers his time as a co-facilitator in Ann Smolin's group, has also been a font of wisdom and knowledge. His ongoing contribution is gratefully appreciated.

Contents

Life must go on, if only for the sake of those who are left, and, what is more, it is our duty to learn to enjoy it again. For what do we regret for those untimely dead, but the opportunity to live with enjoyment? If we are able to give proper meaning and honor to their death, and our grief, we must enjoy the life we, and not they, are privileged to have.

FAY WELDON
The Hearts and Lives of Men

Introduction

Whenever Richard Cory went down town,
We people on the pavement looked at him:
He was a gentlemen from sole to crown,
Clean favored and imperially slim.

And he was always quietly arrayed
And he was always human when he talked;
But still he fluttered pulses when he said,
"Good morning," and he glittered when he walked.

And he was rich—yes, richer than a king—
And admirably schooled in every grace:
In fine, we thought that he was everything
To make us wish that we were in his place.

So on we worked, and waited for the light,
And went without the meat, and cursed the bread;
And Richard Cory, one calm summer night,
Went home and put a bullet through his head.

EDWIN ARLINGTON ROBINSON

Every year 30,000 people end their lives in suicide. They are not just statistical numbers but are husbands, wives, mothers, fathers, sisters, brothers, children, friends, lovers. . . . Why this happens to them and what precedes their deaths has been studied and written about extensively, but what happens afterward to those who are left behind has been given far less attention. If you have experienced that terrible moment in which your joy in living has been suddenly eclipsed by learning that someone you loved has committed suicide, you are a survivor of suicide, another kind of victim of suicide. This book is written for you.

In this book the ambiguous terms *suicide survivor* and *survivor of suicide* or the shortened form *survivor* refer to those who have lost someone they care about to death by suicide. These terms are not used to describe someone who has survived an attempted suicide. When you become a survivor of suicide you are left a painful legacy, not one you chose, but one that was bequeathed to you when someone you loved took the path of suicide. Suicide creates *side effects,* those feelings and occurrences that frequently happen to the survivors. Through the actions of a loved one you have become a victim of these feelings. This book is about side effects and is written for you who may be experiencing them. It is also written for your friends and others who care about you so that they can have an idea of what you are going through and how they may be helpful to you.

What You've Probably Been Going Through

For some, the moment of becoming a suicide survivor is indelibly etched in memory with every excruciating detail clearly recalled, whereas for others, it is obscured in the haze of confused, numb shock. While each individual becomes a suicide survivor in his or her own way, there are predictable phases of pain that most survivors experience sooner or later. Along with the grief and depression of mourning, you will probably feel the self-reproach of guilt, the self-effacement of shame, as well as a helpless rage for what you have lost. You may torture yourself with repetitive interrogations of "What if . . . ?" and "Why didn't we . . . ?" along with the mournful background refrain, "If only. . . ." Underlying the whole cacophony of conflicting and painful emotions the endless lament of "why, why, why?" is heard. The feelings come in unexpected waves that sweep over survivors at various times; most survivors eventually feel the full range of emotions associated with this complex mourning.

While longing to forget their traumatic experience, most survivors will reexperience the event instead, through terrifying
dreams that disturb restful sleep. Most aspects of sleep become
problematic. Falling asleep may be as difficult as staying asleep.
Waking excessively early in the morning, deprived of the welcome
escape that peaceful sleep can bring, faced again with obsessive
thoughts, brings an unpleasant start to the day. Intrusive, unbidden
recollections disrupt attempts at concentrated, focused thought
during waking hours. The unwelcome thoughts persist and recur,
thwarting all efforts to suppress them.

The ability to perform one's usual tasks is impaired. At the
same time there is a diminished ability to be emotionally re-
sponsive in other ways. The survivor is likely to feel distant from
others and is far less able to be intimately connected than he or
she was in the past. Side effects can be troubled relationships,
stressed marriages, and disruption of normal family life. The use
of drugs and alcohol can increase as do the problems associated
with their use. Survivors may experience increased depression,
may have suicidal thoughts, and may make suicide attempts or
even successful suicides.

Too often survivors mourn alone, fearful of seeking comfort
from friends and family, dreading condemnation. Even those who
have support during the early stages of grief may feel abandoned
as their mourning continues for longer than others can tolerate.

Your wounds can heal, you can recover, but not through the
passage of time alone. We offer you this book and the sharing of
fellow survivors' experiences to help you with your healing and
recovery.

Needing Guidance

For several years we have facilitated support groups for suicide
survivors. What we have heard again and again from those who
have come to speak to us is that they have been searching for
explanations, for answers, for understanding, for help. Survivors,

like others, find it reassuring to find out that they are not alone in what they have experienced and felt. Frequently, they have not known where to turn. Survivors and their friends have often looked for helpful reading and have been surprised at how little is available. This book has been written in response to that need.

An Invitation

This book, then, is your invitation to rejoin the community of your fellow human beings, none of whom is immune to suffering. It is an invitation that is written in the words of those who have preceded you in surviving suicide and have struggled until they healed. We offer you the helping hand and encouraging presence of their experiences that they have shared with us as they sought to ease their pain and speed their healing. Their words, more than ours, are the source of your hope.

That this book is the story of many other survivors is your first message of comfort: *You are not alone.* Others have preceded you in this ordeal. Many others are struggling through it now. Sad to say, many more will continue to enter the world of survivors. But you, for now, can use this book to focus on yourself. You may find comfort and hope in the testimony of fellow sufferers, fellow mourners. You can learn what they experienced and suffered, thought and felt, so that you can become a true survivor, alive and well once again.

We do not speak to you as professional researchers or theorists but as facilitators of support groups for survivors. We call ourselves facilitators, from the Latin word *facilis,* meaning "easy." We certainly cannot make the lot of suicide survivors easy, but we can ease their suffering and make easier the healing process of growth and recovery.

We do not claim the title of *leaders* in our groups because we do not lead, either by example or by direction; we are *facilitators*—we explore alongside those whom we try to help. Through this book, you can explore with us as we retrace earlier journeys. When we began these survivor groups we had no hard and fast answers, no shortcuts we could map out. We groped our way with survivors through the morass of their suffering and the gloom of their despair.

What we offer in this book are the routes taken and the conclusions reached by the survivors with whom we worked, as well as their painful detours and the roadblocks along the way. We tell you what they suffered, how they searched for answers, and how they moved toward healing. We offer you the benefit of their experience and their hard-won wisdom, and the understanding we have gained with them. Rarely have we heard any guilt, any self-reproach, or any "If only . . ." from a suicide survivor that has not already been spoken by countless other survivors.

You have probably hidden your loss and pain, feeling shame among friends and strangers. This book invites you into the company of those before whom you need feel no shame. It brings you into the community of those who have suffered the same self-accusation. It lets you know how many others have dreaded the suspected but unspoken condemnation of their neighbors who may blame them for driving their loved one to suicide.

Through the words and experiences of many survivors of suicide, and through our many experiences of helping them with their recovery, we hope to help you learn a few lessons both profound and simple: *You are not alone, you are not to blame, and you are not doomed. You suffer as many others have, and like them you can not only heal and continue to live but you can enjoy life once again.*

How Many Survivors Are There?

It is very conservative to estimate that six to eight people are strongly affected by each of the 30,000 suicides that take place in America each year. At least a quarter of a million Americans become survivors of suicide. Since many of them feel the pain and carry the scars of their loss for years, there are millions of people in this country suffering the aftermath of a suicide. Not only for them is this book written but also for all of their friends and family, who might wish to help them during their distress. All of those people also become survivors of suicide indirectly, when their lives are changed because someone dear to them languishes in depression or isolation in the aftermath of a suicide.

But Why a Book?

This book is the compilation of the experiences shared with us in our facilitating of support groups for suicide survivors over several years. We believe that such groups are an invaluable therapeutic, curative process for suicide survivors. Why then do we attempt to distill these experiences from the vital process of group dynamics into the written word?

We have no doubt that there are many more people looking for help than those who find their way to support groups, for example, those who are not ready to come to a group and those who do not have a nearby support group. These are the people we want to reach with this book.

Many of you will not be able to find a suicide survivor support group to join because there are not that many groups, not nearly as many as are needed. Some support groups are facilitated by mental health professionals like ourselves, but this is not an area into which professionals have rushed to enter. Even mental health professionals have their own fears and prejudices about suicide. Neither of us, as we shall elaborate, undertook facilitating these support groups without reluctance.

Many people, including some mental health professionals, are unconsciously afraid to get to know survivors. It is comfortable for them to maintain a belief that survivors are somehow a different breed from the rest of us. It is easy for them to believe that the survivor was implicated in the suicide of his or her loved one. It is comforting for them to regard survivors as unlike themselves, so they can feel safe that "suicide doesn't happen in families like ours." However, when a survivor becomes a known person, this belief becomes impossible to maintain. It becomes far less clear why one family loses a loved one to suicide while another with no fewer troubles does not.

Suicide challenges most psychological theories of personality and development. None as yet has been able to account adequately for suicide. It is hard for a professional to face survivors without a solid explanation for why this happened. It makes a professional wonder if he could have spotted the potential suicide better than his colleagues who did not, and if he had suspected it, could he have acted to prevent it. He is also aware that suicides may repeat in families, which means that by working with survivors he is dealing with clients who themselves present a high risk for potential suicide. Many professionals avoid working with high-risk groups.

But perhaps the main reason professionals may be reluctant to work with survivors is that they know how deep the pain must be that survivors suffer. What can they offer someone who has lost a child, a spouse, or a parent to suicide? How can they alleviate the aching guilt, the wrenching loss, the recurrent self-recriminations? How can they restore confidence in a survivor's ability to go on living? How can they convince him that he can still laugh and love?

Until recently, the professional community did not address itself to survivor needs. The original survivor groups were facilitated by sensitive and caring people who were themselves survivors, and who were seeking support for their own healing while trying to share the pathways to healing that they discovered for themselves. It is not easy for suicide survivors, with all their natural tendencies to hide their experience, to proclaim their identity to the community in a way that would enable them to form a group.

The result is that in many communities, even large and sophisticated ones, suicide survivor support groups may not exist. Ann Smolin's group in the New York suburb of Westchester County is one of the longer-running survivor groups, and it has existed for only nine years. The stimulus for its creation was a wave of teenage suicides in Westchester County. Westchester Jewish Community Services, working with the county, initiated various programs in response to that rash of suicides, and the program to help survivors was part of it.

Such programs have not been the norm, however. Even after the Westchester County survivor group was founded, there was not a single suicide survivor support group in all of New York City, home to seven million people, a beehive of all sorts of therapeutic activities, and a place where you could find a support group for almost any sort of loss or illness imaginable.

About seven years ago, two Brooklyn women lost a close friend to suicide. They felt they needed others in the same situation to help them through their mourning, but they could not find a suicide survivor support group any closer than a distant New Jersey suburb. They made the difficult trip and attended that group a few times, but they finally decided to form a support group for survivors in New York. It would not be surprising if you were not able to find a group without traveling a great distance. Their experience is also evidence that survivors can successfully band together to help each other—a course that some of you may be inspired to follow. In chapter 13, we offer information on organizing a suicide survivor support group.

Many survivors have suffered in silence and isolation, which is most poignantly illustrated by the survivors who have come to our groups twenty or more years after the suicide of someone close. A number of them have said that in all those years they were never able to reveal to anyone that the death was a suicide, let alone face their complex feelings about it.

For many who have struggled with the pain of suicide survival totally alone, it is a great relief just to be present at one support meeting. It is a tremendous relief just to learn that there are so many other survivors and that they feel so many of the same things. All the emotions that had been previously shrouded with self-reproaches—"I feel like a terrible person saying this . . ." or "I don't know if anyone else ever reacted this way . . ."—can now be recognized as what many survivors feel. They can be accepted as natural reactions to a very unnatural act.

For you in that lonely grief, struggling to find your way through torment, which is difficult even with ample support, we hope this book can be a vital link. If you have never shared your feelings with anyone and have never had the opportunity to know how other suicide survivors feel, look and listen through the window of this book, as your fellow sufferers struggle along the road to healing. If this book brings even one person out of isolation it is of value.

And Even If There Is a Group Near You . . .

Another way to use this book is to help you take the first step and attend a meeting. Most of the people who have come to our groups have described how difficult it was to come for the first time. Going for the first time to a therapy session or to any group that involves disclosure of strong personal feelings can arouse intense anxiety. Thus, many people would like to know what they are getting into before they take that bold first step. In telling the experiences of survivors with whom we have worked, this book will give you a sense of what the groups are like.

There is another group of survivors to whom this book is addressed: those who are survivors of suicide in every painful sense of the word but who are not relatives. Although most of those who come to suicide survivor support groups are close relatives of the person who committed suicide—parents, siblings, sons and daughters, spouses, lovers—there are many others who suffer just as intensely, even if their relationship with the suicide victim was not as intimate.

Anyone who is personally touched by the death is a survivor. If you are a teacher or a neighbor or a co-worker, you are not out of place in a survivor support group. What defines a survivor of suicide is not the degree of closeness to the individual but the intensity of the reaction to the loss. We assure you that if you are suffering over a suicide, you have a place in a survivor support group. For now, let this book be an opening for you into the community of survivors.

And What This Book Is Not

Despite the endless litany of "why" from survivors, we do not try to delve into the motivations for suicide. Indeed, one point we make repeatedly is that there is almost never only one reason for a suicide. Every suicide is *multidetermined,* that is, it is the product of a number of motivating factors interacting in a particularly fatal mix.

This book is about the living, the survivors, rather than about those who committed suicide. It concerns itself with understanding why people kill themselves only to the extent that doing so helps the survivors through their ordeal. You may have shed, and may continue to shed, countless tears for the dead. Our goal is not only to help you go on living but to help you live life as fully and as rewardingly as possible.

This book is also not meant to replace either a support group or therapy. We believe that almost all suicide survivors could benefit from a support group. No book should ever replace the actual sharing of feelings with those who share your pain. No book can replace therapy for those who may need it. We do help you determine if and when you may be in need of some therapeutic help.

For now, enter with us into the world of suicide survivors—people sharing their pain and trying to find resolution for their grief. We hope you will find much here that will help you. If there are some feelings or experiences with which you cannot identify, that is fine. Do not feel that you should be able to relate to everything that every other survivor has been through. Each survivor, like each suicide, is unique. Follow the advice of Al-Anon: "Take that which you find helpful, and leave the rest behind."

Chapter 1

A Day in
the Life of a
Survivor

Three weeks after his eighteen-year-old son Robbie hung himself, Bill G.'s life began to resume many of its day-to-day routines. He still fluctuated between agonizing grief and other periods where numbness set in, and he went through his daily activities like a robot.

One of these days began with Bill waking at 5:00 A.M. He then sank back on his pillow with relief when he realized this was *not* one of the mornings when he was awakened from a nightmare in which he was seeing Robbie's body hanging in the attic. Many mornings he was drenched with sweat, emerging from a nightmare in which he had been struggling to run to Robbie, believing that if he could just get the body down and release the rope from around Robbie's neck he could somehow breathe life back into his son. However, in these awful dreams he was never able to move quickly; his legs felt leaden and he could barely move them, so that he was tortured by his inability to get to Robbie and save him. On the mornings Bill awoke from these nightmares, he had very bad days, with the dream images flashing back repeatedly.

So at least Bill was numb when he wandered down to the kitchen and sat at the breakfast table this particular Monday morning. Mornings were difficult even on the numb days, though; it was the time of day when Bill felt the least energetic. Monday mornings were even more difficult, as the week of work looming ahead seemed like a huge burden. Before Robbie's death that had never been the case. Bill's work brought him into contact with lots of clients, and he had usually looked ahead with pleasure to the meetings he had scheduled during the coming week. Pleasure in seeing his client-friends used to offset the intense work load Bill carried.

Bill's surviving son Ken, age sixteen, sat down with him at the table and began to pick at a small breakfast, his once voracious teenage appetite gone. Since Robbie's death, Ken was subdued, and it was especially apparent at mealtime. He now took small portions and left more on his plate than he consumed.

This morning Ken interrupted his half-hearted munching on a slice of toast to ask his dad if he could use the family car to drive four other kids to a rock concert that night. Bill replied irritably, "You should have more sense than to think about going to a concert on a school night, especially since you've gotten behind in your schoolwork since ... over the past few weeks." "Gee thanks, Dad," Ken snapped back. "I try to do something so I don't feel like I'm living in a morgue and you bug me about schoolwork." Leaving the half-eaten slice of toast on his plate, Ken disappeared from the room, slamming the door behind him.

Bill sat at the table, his own appetite gone, stung by Ken's use of the word *morgue*. Many words related to death hit Bill like a lash whenever he heard them. He managed a rueful smile at the thought that typically, if Ken were going to storm out of the kitchen in some adolescent outburst, he not only would have taken the slice of toast along but would have scooped up a few more pieces to fuel his exuberant energy. It just reminded Bill that there wasn't much exuberance in the family since that day.

Bill continued to sit at the table, food forgotten, lost in thought. He knew that one reason he had jumped on Ken about going to a concert on a school night was to avoid having to answer Ken's request for the car. Bill was avoiding making any decisions, especially about Ken. Since Robbie's death, Bill had been deluged with doubts about what he and his wife could have done differently with Rob, and how they should have handled various situations.

Bill feared that some of his decisions about what was best for Robbie had been wrong. He wondered which of them might have contributed to Robbie's suicide and wished he could take back some arguments and some decisions he had made that had sent Robbie into a fit of anger. "If only I'd been more flexible, maybe it wouldn't have happened." Just as quickly, Bill sometimes blamed himself for the opposite: "If only I'd been more strict and set more rigid rules, he might have felt more secure and he wouldn't have done it."

The upshot was that Bill was very uncomfortable with making decisions about Ken now, especially when they might involve Ken's safety or well-being. Bill had so tormented himself about all the possibly wrong decisions he had made about what Robbie should do that he felt no confidence in his ability to make any decisions about Ken.

Having lost one child, Bill was terrified of losing Ken. Thus, he wanted to protect Ken, and keeping Ken close to home and away from any "dangerous" activities like driving seemed to be the safest course. This, combined with Bill's distrust of his ability to make good decisions, left him feeling that the less Ken did on his own, the better.

Another feeling crept into Bill's awareness and aroused anger. "How could Ken want to go to a rock concert only three weeks after Robbie's death? Isn't he still grieving over his brother's death?

Doesn't he have any feelings? How can he be running around as if nothing had happened?"

Ken was seething with resentment as he walked to school. He sensed his Dad's withdrawal into his grief, but experienced it as hurt and abandonment. Ken wasn't verbalizing his feelings much, but he did feel a great void as well as confusion. He avoided looking closely at his feelings for the time being. However, he would have liked the support of knowing his father was there for him and tuned in to his feelings. Instead, he saw his father consumed by mourning for Robbie.

Ken was left feeling, "What's the matter with me? Aren't you glad you still have me? Can't you take a few minutes away from your gloom and let me know that you still enjoy having *me* around? Would it matter to you if I killed myself too? Would it take *that* to remind you that I *was* still around?"

Back at home, Bill pushed his chair away from the breakfast table as he heard his wife, Sally, coming down the stairs. Since Rob's death, it was typical of Sally to sleep late. Unlike Bill, who found sleep elusive, Sally went to bed early, seemed to sleep soundly, and got up much later than usual.

Bill was irritated as Sally came down to the kitchen. He resented that because of her lack of energy she had done hardly any cooking or cleaning over the past three weeks. Bill had pitched in and done as much as he could, but he felt burdened by the extra work. The emotional burdens Sally was placing on him were even greater. She hated to be alone, but whenever he was with her, Sally talked endlessly about Robbie. Bill had plenty of tortured thoughts of his own about their son and just didn't want to listen to Sally; she made him feel like he wanted to escape.

There was a deeper reason for Bill's anger toward Sally, which he only partly admitted to himself. He had tormented himself with questions of how they should have done things differently with Robbie, and Sally had not emerged guiltless from this inquisition. Bill secretly blamed her for coddling Robbie and making him too much of a mama's boy. Bill felt she had made Robbie so dependent on her that he couldn't handle difficulties on his own. Bill still loved Sally, though, and he didn't always believe his conclusions about her culpability, so he wouldn't bring up any of these feelings to her.

For the moment, Bill avoided dealing with Sally. "Sorry, honey, I'm late for a meeting," he said. He put his coffee cup in the sink, grabbed his suit jacket and, giving Sally a peck on the cheek, was out the door before she could say a word.

As he drove away, Bill realized that he did not have the catalogs of new computer equipment he wanted to show his clients. Bill had gotten them a month in advance of the equipment's introduction date and had stored them away in his attic until it was time to start showing them. Now he hated to go near the attic and often completely forgot about the catalogs.

When Bill arrived at his client's office, he went to the data processing unit and greeted the company's four-member data processing staff. Since he visited this department every six to eight weeks, he had gotten to know Tom, the department supervisor, fairly well. Tom called out "hello" as Bill entered, and then added, as he had other times, "How have you been? How's the family?"

In most social situations, questions like that are little more than elaborations on "hello," perhaps a little more personal since they acknowledge some familiarity—a friendly gesture but not a particularly serious one. This day, Bill could feel the color drain from his face as he stood speechless in response to Tom's query. A solid blow to his midsection couldn't have felt more painful. His silence drew the attention of the other three staff members, and Bill was acutely aware of four pairs of eyes suddenly regarding him with uncertainty.

Taking a deep breath to steady himself, Bill struggled to collect his thoughts and force some words from his mouth. In a shaky voice he said, "We had a real tragedy, Tom. We lost our son." Tom looked shocked. Then, as a stunned silence enveloped the room, Tom said softly, "That's awful, Bill! How did it happen?"

In the back of his mind, Bill had known there would be chance encounters when he would meet someone who didn't know about the suicide, but with whom the news was bound to emerge. Consumed with dealing with his own anguish, he had put off any further planning about how he would handle the situation. Now it had exploded in his face and he hadn't thought about what he wanted to say or how people were likely to react.

Bill was like a swimmer suddenly swept under the surface by a huge wave, trying to make his way back to the surface. All his shame, grief, rage, and confusion swept over him as he tried to formulate an answer to Tom's question. Finally, he just blurted out, "Robbie killed himself."

Now it was Tom who was speechless. One staff member's mouth literally dropped open. Another suddenly averted his glance and self-consciously began to shuffle some printouts on his desk. Tom finally managed to recover some of his composure, and again said, "That's terrible! How is Sally taking it?" Bill managed to mumble some platitudes like, "As well as can be expected," and Tom veered off into what a terrible shock it had been when his brother-in-law's nineteen-year-old son was killed in a car accident two years earlier, and how the family was still having trouble accepting it.

Tom and Bill exchanged further commiserations about the shock of sudden death and how terrible the death of a young person was. The other staff immersed themselves in their work, and though Bill didn't know them as well as Tom, he sensed they were avoiding him. Even Tom, though he was obviously sympathetic and trying to offer comfort, never mentioned the fact that Robbie had taken his own life. After a few minutes of such talk, Bill forced a wan smile and said, "You just have to try and keep going. . . . So, how's the conversion to the new system working out?" He sensed relief in Tom as they suddenly talked very intensely about all the details of the new computer workstations.

Driving back to his office afterward, Bill couldn't help remembering the stunned and awkward silence after he said that Robbie had killed himself. He began to imagine what thoughts had gone through Tom's mind, but without realizing it clearly, he turned his attention away from the question. Suddenly he felt angry, but he had no idea why. Only many weeks later, when the memory of this day came back to him, did he realize the momentary thought that had flashed through his mind. He had imagined Tom telling his wife about Robbie's suicide, and her replying, "Bill and Sally seemed like nice people—it's hard to imagine their family being so troubled. I guess you can never tell about people." That thought pointed the finger too much, placed too much stigma on the family, for Bill to have let himself face it at the time it first entered his mind. Of course it was a product of *his* imagination, illustrating the interaction between the survivor's own guilt and the real stigma attached to suicide.

The thought of Tom talking to his wife when he got home that night, plus Bill's need to avoid the contents of that imagined conversation, turned Bill's thoughts to the time he had first met Tom's wife. It was at a company Christmas party. This recollection made Bill think of the setting, with a huge Christmas tree in the middle of the company cafeteria. He felt himself break out into a cold sweat as he tried to picture what the next Christmas would be like with his own family—*with Robbie gone.*

That thought came to a sudden halt as Bill realized the traffic ahead of him was stopped. He slammed on the brakes, barely stopping short of the car in front of him. His heart pounding with anxiety, both from the near accident and the anguished images that had started to form in his mind, Bill leaned back in the seat and felt drained. He abandoned the plan to go back to the office to finish up some paperwork and decided to just go home.

Does this sound familiar to you? Although this one hypothetical example is a synthesis of many survivors' experiences, you can probably identify with some of the situations. Like Bill, have you felt overwhelmed by some situations and feelings without even realizing why? Have you tried to just muddle through in spite of all the pain and confusion you are feeling?

If you're nodding your head to these questions, that's probably why you are looking at this book right now. You are wishing for a way out of the feelings. You are wishing you could feel like a normal person again. *You can!* This book can help you not because the authors have brilliant solutions or clever advice but because we have observed how dozens of other suicide survivors have found their way out of the morass of pain and isolation. We have helped other survivors to help each other with that healing, and we will share with you what they shared with us and with each other.

Let us give you a quick survey of the problems Bill faced—and that you may be facing. We illustrate some, give names to the major issues, and indicate where in this book we deal with a specific problem.

First of all, there is a name for the whole pattern of difficulties suicide survivors face. In the diagnostic terminology used by mental health clinicians, it is *posttraumatic stress disorder.* This may seem like a digression into psychiatric jargon, but it is important to realize that what may seem like a confusing array of difficulties is, in fact, a well-known and well-recognized constellation of symptoms experienced by many people.

The *Diagnostic Manual of the American Psychiatric Association* lists the following criteria for a diagnosis of posttraumatic stress disorder:

A. Existence of a recognizable stressor that would evoke significant symptoms of distress in almost anyone
B. Reexperiencing of the trauma as evidenced by at least one of the following:
   1. recurrent and intrusive recollections of the event
   2. recurrent dreams of the event
   3. sudden acting or feeling as if the trauma were recurring because of an association with a thought or an external situation
C. Numbing of responsiveness to or reduced involvement with the external world, as shown by at least one of the following:

1. markedly diminished interest in one or more significant activities
2. feeling of detachment or estrangement from others
3. constricted emotions

D. At least two of the following symptoms that were not
present before the trauma:
1. hyperalertness or exaggerated startled response
2. sleep disturbance
3. guilt about surviving when someone else has not, or
about behavior required for survival
4. memory impairment or trouble concentrating
5. avoidance of activities that arouse recollection of the
traumatic event
6. intensification of symptoms by exposure to events that
symbolize or represent the traumatic event

If you are suffering the pain of surviving suicide, you probably meet these criteria. Our hypothetical survivor, Bill, certainly does. We hope it is a helpful beginning for you to know that there is a name for what you are going through. And not only does the syndrome have a name but there are ways of treating it if it is not alleviated by the normal process of mourning and healing.

Posttraumatic stress disorder, of course, is not a pattern of symptoms afflicting suicide survivors only. It can follow any sort of traumatic event, which only underscores the fact that survivors' pain has much in common with a wide range of human suffering. Suicide survivors' pain is also unique, though. Thus, this book is about and for suicide survivors only.

It is a common fear of survivors who have not had the opportunity to share their feelings that they are alone in feeling what they do. It is always a great relief to find that other survivors go through the same things, and the appendix lists support groups that may help you. Based on the experiences of Bill and his family, let us outline a few of the main issues for you.

Depression is one of the main components of survivor pain. Bill and his family exhibit many symptoms of depression. Bill's waking in the early morning and his lack of energy in the morning, his wife's neglect of her usual household chores, and his son Ken's loss of appetite are all typical manifestations of depression. Chapter 6 will help you recognize what parts of your difficulty are due to depression. It outlines how some depression is an inevitable reaction to suicide, and how some of it is generally eased by time. The chapter also outlines ways of dealing with other depressive symptoms that may not go away in time.

Guilt is a main component of survivor pain. Guilt is frequently heard in survivors' tortured refrain of "We should have . . . ," "We could have . . . ," and "If only we had. . . ." We can see how Bill is tortured by such self-recrimination and then lets it affect his attitudes toward his wife and son. Chapter 3 deals with guilt. It will help you recognize how guilt is affecting you. Bill's inability to make decisions regarding his surviving son, for instance, is rooted in his guilty self-doubt about how he dealt with Robbie.

A recent article in *The New York Times,* "Why Primo Levi Need Not Have Died," by novelist William Styron, deals with the suicide of Levi, an Italian writer. Styron speaks of his own experience with severe depression, including suicidal feelings that led him to voluntarily admit himself to a psychiatric hospital. Styron concludes that if only Levi had been recognized as depressed and had been hospitalized, his life could have been saved.

Although hospitalization or another form of treatment *might* have helped, no one can be sure that any particular treatment would have saved Levi's life. We have had people in our survivor support groups relate how a loved one committed suicide in a psychiatric hospital, saying, "If only I hadn't let them hospitalize her . . . if only I had cared for her at home. . . ."

Almost always, the "should have" and "if only" statements are not realistic appraisals but only expressions of guilt at not having been omnipotent enough to prevent the suicide. As you read various survivors' accounts in this book, you will learn that what one survivor guiltily feels she "should have" done was, in fact, done before some other person's suicide occurred; that person's survivor is left lamenting "if only I hadn't" done that. Part of escaping the clutches of guilt is recognizing that no one issue, no one person, and thus not *you* alone can ever be the sole cause of a suicide.

Part of Bill's inability to make decisions for his son Ken was dread of possibly losing a second child. This fear of another suicide or another loss by any cause is something you must guard against. It is not so much a realistic fear rising out of your own experience, but it is a reaction common to many survivors. It often leads to smothering overprotection toward surviving family members, such as siblings in the case of an adolescent's suicide. Recognizing the underlying fear of another loss and verbalizing it, is an essential ingredient in not letting it cripple your judgment.

Bill became angry toward Ken for wanting to go to a rock concert so soon after Robbie's death; he took that as a sign that Ken was not grieving for his brother. Do not make the mistake of assuming that others will mourn or deal with their grief in the same way you do. Different people handle their grieving in different ways. Ken may have needed to go to the concert with his friends to assure himself that he was still committed to living and was not depressed as his brother had been.

If you like to make frequent visits to the grave of your brother, you may feel hurt or angry if your father or your sister rarely visits the cemetery. You need to try and understand that visiting the grave may be a very different experience for the two of you. You may feel close to your brother when you visit the grave and you may feel able to communicate with him, whereas for your father or sister a visit to the cemetery may serve only as a reminder of death. They may get in touch with the memory of your brother by some other route.

We also saw Ken was hurt by his father's withdrawal into his own grief. Ken could have benefited from his Dad's support and understanding to help sort out his own feelings, but Bill was too preoccupied with his own pain. If you have lost a sibling to suicide, you may feel that you have also lost your parents if they are not emotionally available. You may feel resentment if they remain overwhelmed by grief for too long a time. You may feel that you, who are still there for them, are less important than your sibling who is gone. Chapter 11 elaborates on these issues and suggests ways to cope with them. Three other chapters will deal with the particular family issues in case of suicide by a parent (chapter 8), a child (chapter 9), or a spouse (chapter 10).

One of Ken's resentful thoughts about his father's preoccupation with Robbie's death was, "Would it matter to you if I killed myself?" It is a fact that survivors of suicide are at greater risk of committing suicide and are more likely to find themselves contemplating suicide in the aftermath of their loss, even if they did not previously. This subject is dealt with in chapter 7. You should recognize that just as surely as you are not doomed, you are in greater danger. You must monitor the seriousness of these impulses when you feel them and learn to recognize if you need help with them. Chapter 7 gives warning signals.

Chapter 7 also discusses serious risk-taking behavior, or other things that place you in danger. We saw how Bill's preoccupation with his thoughts about Robbie distracted him from his driving and almost got him into an accident.

Bill was secretly blaming Sally for some of the ways she had dealt with Robbie that he felt could have contributed to Robbie's suicide. He only half admitted these to himself and did not discuss them with Sally. You may find yourself doing this, or you may be on the receiving end of blaming attitudes from someone else. This sort of blaming or scapegoating is discussed throughout the book. Such outlooks may be dividing your family at the time when you need support the most.

Those who are doing the blaming need to examine their feelings. Frequently, blaming is an extension onto someone else of "If only . . ." thinking and is usually as unrealistic as when directed at oneself. When these attitudes are present, it is better to try and talk them through than to keep them under wraps, where they are sensed but can never be resolved. This is a case where outside professional assistance may be required to defuse the intensity of the feelings.

All of the chapters touch on fear of other people's attitudes and dread of having to talk about the suicide. Once again, one of the most important lessons for you to learn is that almost any feelings you have had about other people's attitudes will have been shared by numerous survivors. We offer suggestions on how to anticipate awkward situations and how to handle them.

Chapter 2

Denial:

"It Can't Be!"

In his autobiography, Russell Baker recalls when he was five years old and his father died. His playmate told him, "Your father's dead!" Russell could only reply "He is not," so that they quickly got into a cross fire of "He is too!" and "He is not!" Many adults, confronted with news of a shocking death—and suicide is always a shock even if it may have been anticipated—react with a similar sort of "he is not dead" to protect themselves from devastating pain and emotional disorientation.

Professionals in the field use the term *denial* to describe this psychological response in which the self shields itself from feelings it cannot bear. What the self is actually saying is, "Reality is too painful, so I won't believe it." Denial is a blunt, primitive defense mechanism that develops fairly early in childhood. Since it does not rely on the mind's more sophisticated skills, it doesn't do a particularly good job at camouflaging reality. It simply enables the conscious self to announce, "I am not hurting."

Denial is a relatively natural way of cushioning us against the shock of death. It insulates us against the jarring impact of having someone who has been a significant part of our world suddenly removed, never to return. In facing the loss of a loved one by suicide, many survivors use denial from the very beginning to avoid being totally swept away by the intensity of the pain.

The Initial Reaction

When the reality that a loved one has killed herself is simply too much to bear, a normal first reaction is to say to yourself, "It can't be so." There are many ways of doing this. Some people avoid hearing the message altogether.

Pauline described how her mind initially refused to accept the news of her husband's death. A doctor from a hospital emergency room telephoned and said, "Your husband has killed himself." Pauline totally blocked the horrible reality of his words, and replied, "What do you mean he killed himself? You mean his heart condition killed him, but that's not the same as killing yourself!" Pauline's response was an extreme form of blocking, as she now realizes. The news of her husband's suicide was so appalling that she had to deny what was being said to her. That denial was the very beginning of her coping with his suicide.

A less dramatic way of not integrating the loss into consciousness is to hear the facts but be unable to digest them. Melanie received a call from her friend, Lois, who said that her husband Sam had just died. He had been seriously ill, so the death was not a great surprise. After offering condolences, Melanie hung up the phone and spent a few minutes with her own husband discussing Sam's death. She then concluded, "I guess I'll send a note to Sam and Lois." Even though his death was anticipated, Sam was a dear and lifelong friend and Melanie's unconscious self was not prepared to accept that he was gone. Her denial let him remain with her for a little while longer.

Layers of Insulation

Despite its limitations as a coping mechanism, denial can be a good friend and valuable helper to the suicide survivor. Although it is psychologically dishonest, it sometimes helps people get through situations they otherwise could not bear. Denial is a way of shutting out part of the trauma and letting us deal with it on our own timetable. When we have mastered or at least become able to face one part of the tragedy, we can set aside denial and see more of the whole picture.

Many facets of suicide become sealed in denial, wrapped layer upon layer around one another. Even after the outer layer of denial dissolves, many additional layers may remain. Sometimes the conscious mind tries to resist the knowledge that a loved one has died by continuing to believe that he is still alive. You may think that you hear him coming back into the house or that you see him walking down a familiar street. You may find yourself starting to pick up the telephone to call the person who has killed himself. Doing these things is perfectly normal for a suicide survivor. This is a point we will repeat: *Doing something that may seem "odd" can be a very natural response when coping with the trauma of death, and especially with the uniquely devastating trauma of suicide.*

Forms of Denial

Even after you absorb the shock of a loved one's death, you may still not be prepared to accept that she took her own life. You may try to believe that the death is something other than a suicide. There are many different ways survivors attempt to do this. Some ways are harmless, whereas others are more noxious because they are serious distortions of reality that interfere with grieving and healing. The more serious problem-causing ones are examples of denial being a poor coping mechanism and creating more problems than it solves.

Benign Denial

One of the more common—and benign—forms of suicide denial is the wish to believe that somehow the death was not a suicide. Survivors may cling to a hope that it will turn out that the medical report was a mistake, that there was an accident, or that the person died of a heart attack. In most cases, this hope gradually fades in the days or weeks that follow. No harm is done; facing the truth is just delayed.

Mark, age sixteen, killed himself by taking an overdose of pills and cutting his wrists. His family tried to believe that while he had taken the drugs deliberately, the overdose was unintentional; this allowed them to see his death as the result of an accidental overdose, and thus not a suicide. This was obviously a flimsy attempt at denial, because it failed to take his cut wrists into account.

Fairly soon Mark's family faced the obvious reality of his suicide and began the process of coming to terms with their feelings about it. They attended a survivor support group and worked through many of their difficulties about facing their son's (or brother's) decision to take his own life. Their denial of suicide did no great harm. It sidetracked them from grieving, but it also bought them time. It let them adjust to the crushing reality of his sudden death. Only after they had made some initial accommodation to that loss could they move on to face the additional agony of knowing that he made a voluntary choice to end his life.

Denial Hindering Healing

Other survivors collude with one another to create a complicated system of denial that actually impedes the recovery process. Mort was a stockbroker whose family knew he was facing some serious financial problems, probably involving criminal acts. They were shocked when they learned he had shot himself and they professed to believe that he had been murdered in retaliation for having given bad investment advice. This was not altogether implausible, but there was not much evidence for it.

The family put considerable time and emotional energy into constructing theories about how Mort had been murdered. They created serious distortions of reality and kept themselves from dealing with what actually happened and with their own feelings of loss at his death. They were so intent on finding evidence for their theory that he had been murdered that they did not even begin the work of mourning his death. Once they were able to face his suicide, they could begin to mourn his loss.

Blame as Denial

Assigning blame to someone else for the suicide is another way of denying the choice someone made to take his own life. Blame is often traded back and forth within the surviving family. Mothers blame fathers, in-laws blame husbands or wives, and siblings blame parents. At other times blaming involves some outside party, such as the owners of a building from which a person jumped to his death. All forms of blame can be destructive and may interfere with the grief work that must be accomplished if one is to heal.

Blaming an outside party, for instance, can evolve into years of legal wrangling. It becomes psychologically unhealthy when it prevents the survivors from dealing with their loss realistically. By staying angry at an outsider you lose the opportunity to work on your feelings about the person who has died.

The persistence of intense anger over a number of years is

often a clue that denial is at work. When anger is legitimate, it tends to diminish over time. It is healthy to let go of anger so that one is not consumed by it. When anger rages unabated, it is often misdirected anger that cannot be alleviated with the passing of time because the person is not facing the true source and target of her angry feelings.

It is particularly painful to watch family members blaming one another for their loved one's suicide. It does not help anyone cope with the suicide and it poisons relationships among the survivors. One of the most common scenarios involves the parents of an adult who has committed suicide and that person's spouse. This blame is particularly apt to happen if there was conflict in the marriage before the suicide.

Both the parents and the surviving spouse are, of course, facing their own agonies. If they are like almost all other suicide survivors, they are already questioning themselves about where they went wrong, what clues they missed, and what they could have done to prevent the suicide. Such self-accusations are, as you know only too well, extremely potent and torturing. Having them leveled at you by relatives is all the more devastating.

It can just as easily happen that a surviving spouse or lover attributes the suicide to difficulties in the victim's relationship with her parents. Whichever way the blaming is directed, the person who is the object of it has her own guilty feelings reinforced. In addition, relationships that might have been mutually helpful to healing and recovery are sundered and become toxic.

Beyond the direct loss of these relationships to the parties involved, there is spillover conflict within the already traumatized extended family. The valuable relationships between grandparents and their grandchildren are often ruptured, sometimes severed, when there is bitter conflict between the children's parents and the grandparents. Thus, an additional element of pain, conflict, and loss is introduced in a family that has already suffered a grievous injury.

Even less close relationships can become problematic if members of the extended family begin taking sides in the blaming contest. That self-destructive act can sow a legacy of bitterness and resentment that persists for years.

Conscious Denial

Perhaps the most common form of denial practiced by survivors is hiding the fact that the death was a suicide. The wish to do this relates to the shame attached to suicide, which we will discuss in chapter 4.

Many survivors either avoid discussing the cause of death, or they actively disguise it, for instance, stating that the person had a heart attack. Members of a suicide survivor group discussing an obituary stating that the cause of death was a *"presumed* heart attack" instantly made the assumption that such a vague statement pointed toward a suicide death. They had seen such a variety of means of disguising suicide in their own situations that they were inclined to suspect it in any evasive statement.

Survivors often feel that by denying that a death was a suicide they are protecting the memory of their loved one. They believe that such denial is also a way to avoid letting the world know that there were troubles in their family. They fear that to admit a suicide took place is to expose personal agonies for the titillation of others.

Denial—
Just the First Response

Denial is often the first way of handling feelings about suicide. Denial is primarily a short-term avoidance of unbearable pain. Something too horrible to imagine is suddenly presented as reailty, and the mind feels no other choice than to refuse to be aware of it. Pain is a key ingredient of the process. Since mourning is a process of adjusting to a painful loss, until the pain can be faced, the mourning cannot take place. After denial, the self uses other approaches to the pain of surviving suicide, as we shall discuss in subsequent chapters.

Chapter 3

Guilt:

"We Should Have . . .

We Could Have . . ."

The worst torture is thinking, "I could have done something to prevent it." Much of the talk in survivor support groups concerns the motivations of the suicide: "Why did he do it?" "What was she feeling?" "What could she have been thinking of?" While this questioning reflects a real wish to understand the feelings and motivations of the person who has killed himself in order to come to peace with the act, just as often it is an attempt to figure out what you, the survivor, could and should have done differently.

Survivors often believe, "If only I had stayed with him (or married him, or made love to him, or not insisted on moving to my own place, or . . .), he would still be alive." There is no way of knowing what would have happened. Even if you had done whatever it is you torment yourself for not doing, and even if you did deter the suicide from happening, that is hardly the same as preventing it altogether.

Take off the Guilt-Colored Glasses!

Deena came to our group after her daughter had killed herself. Her daughter had been quite depressed for some time, and Deena was spending a lot of time with her, trying to help her out of her depression. In our group, more than once, Deena discussed the nature of depression at some length and reviewed the onset of her daughter's depression. Deena castigated herself for not realizing the depth and the severity of her daughter's depression: "If only I had understood how depressed she was, and the seriousness of it, I would have had her hospitalized."

Eva's story was a far more effective reply to Deena's self-rebuke than anything a group facilitator might have said. Eva's daughter, like Deena's, had been depressed for a number of years, partly in reaction to her father's alcoholism, and partly, Eva felt, in response to Eva's own battle with cancer, which had gone on through much of her daughter's adolescence. Eva's daughter had been hospitalized. In fact, she was a patient in one of New York's better-known hospitals when she hung herself with the belt of the robe that the hospital gave her. (Eva did take note that in another hospital, where her daughter had been, patients were given robes without belts as a suicide precaution.)

Despite any lapse in judgment she might believe the hospital showed by providing her daughter with what became the immediate instrument of her suicide, Eva's most intense blaming was reserved for herself. Her self-accusation focused on her having been at fault in letting her daughter be hospitalized. With hindsight, Eva felt that she should have kept her daughter at home and spent more time with her, rather than heeding the psychiatrist's advice to distance herself from her daughter.

What added impact and poignancy to Deena and Eva's inventories of self-doubt was that they were delivered at the same survivor group meeting. Deena faulted herself for not having had her daughter hospitalized, while Eva regretted having agreed to let her daughter be hospitalized. Deena and Eva each felt that, had they taken the opposite course, their daughters would still be alive.

When Even Hindsight Isn't 20/20

The common saying is that we all have 20/20 vision in hindsight, but this example of two survivors proves there are exceptions. The problem is that although you can see what you could have done differently before the suicide, it is not clear that you could have permanently prevented a suicide from happening—or even that it would have been prevented at that moment.

Had you taken an alternate course of action, maybe the suicide would have been put off until the next day, or the next month, or even the next year. And, yes, if it had been put off, maybe some more therapy or medication might have been attempted, and maybe the suicide really would have been averted altogether. *But maybe it could not have been—and there is no way of knowing!* What it is possible to know is that whatever course you fault yourself for not having taken, there is someone else blaming himself for having taken that same course.

This is the immensely important lesson of Deena and Eva's stories. No one can ever be sure that a different choice would have prevented the suicide. Why convict yourself on the basis of insufficient evidence when, indeed, no compelling evidence can ever be obtained.

I'm Guilty! . . . Yes, But . . .

Paul laments having owned the gun with which his son shot himself; he is right, of course, that if he had not owned a gun, and had not kept it in his apartment, his son could not have shot himself with it. But he could have taken an overdose of pills or slashed his wrists. Yes, Paul may reply, but had he done one of those things, we might have been able to get him to a hospital and save him; those things aren't always fatal. Right again, but he also could have jumped out the apartment window and suffered a certain death. He even might have obtained a gun in some other way. Those who are intent on committing suicide find a way to do so. The point is, the arguments, the "if only" suppositions and the "yes, but" retorts, can go on forever.

Blaming Before the Fact

Many suicide survivors were embarked on a guilt trip before the suicide ever took place. Many people threaten suicide, either verbally or by their actions, long before they take their own lives. Many of you, having been faced with evidence of such suicidal ideas or impulses in your loved ones, took on a good deal of responsibility for preventing the suicide. Very understandably, you lived in terror of your loved one's taking her own life. Just as understandably, though not as logically, you may have concluded that you would be responsible if she ever did kill herself.

Al is a good example. His mother was an alcoholic through much of his growing-up years. On one occasion he witnessed her menacing a relative with a knife. More often her destructiveness was directed at herself. One night she ran out of their home and attempted to throw herself in front of a car. Like many children of alcoholic parents (a category into which many suicide survivors fall), Al tried to look out for his mother. He took on the responsibility of stopping her from killing herself. For years, his biggest fear was that she would finally kill herself, and that he would be overwhelmed with guilt.

Al's story has a relatively happy ending. His mother did not kill herself. Even so, the memory of his dread of her possible suicide, and the terror he lived with for at least seven years, are among the most intense emotional experiences of his life.

An objective person hearing Al's story can empathize with his agony but can also recognize that he put this burden undeservedly on himself. Any objective observer can see that he was really powerless to control his mother's behavior. Nonetheless, many survivors take on this guilt.

The Ultimate Form of Blackmail

A threat of suicide is the ultimate form of emotional blackmail. It is used as a desperate attempt to control another's behavior. Many of you were explicitly threatened with suicide before the act was done. "I'll kill myself if you don't marry me!" or "I'll kill myself if you leave me!" are two of the most common forms that this threat can take. When such threats are made it is an indication that a real relationship is not viable. If you are threatened with suicide to make you commit to the relationship, you are in for endless trouble.

After you are involved in the relationship, when you have emotional bonds to the person, the dilemma is much more complicated. Now you can't walk away from the relationship without risking that which you fear most. What you should realize is that someone who can threaten you in this way is insensitive to you and your feelings. It may well be that he is too depressed or otherwise ill to be capable of sensitivity to you, but clearly he is not attending to your feelings and needs. He is no longer involved in a mutual, caring relationship with you.

We are talking a lot here about guilt that people may feel at the risk or threat of suicide, even when no suicide has taken place. It may be easier to see, in those cases, how it is grossly unfair and unreasonable for anyone to tell someone else that she will be responsible if he kills himself. Also, you are taking on a huge burden if you feel responsible for preventing another's suicide.

For a Verdict of "Not Guilty"!

We could go on endlessly reciting specific "could've," "should've," and "would've" ruminations that we have heard from survivors in our support groups. There is really no point in doing so. The most fundamental statement we can make is: *You did not cause the suicide, and you are not responsible for it having happened!* The choice someone makes to commit suicide cannot be understood easily. It does not come to pass because of a single event or series of events. Perhaps you had separated from your husband before he committed suicide. Perhaps he even threatened to kill himself if you did not return to him. Did you cause his suicide? *No!* Hundreds of thousands of women separate from their husbands every year. Do all the husbands kill themselves? Of course not—only a minuscule fraction do.

Or perhaps you argued with your teenage daughter, placing some restriction on her before her suicide. Perhaps she even ran out of the room crying, "You're ruining my life. . . . I'm going to kill myself!" Did you cause her suicide? Again, *no!* Arguing with parents is a daily staple of teenage life. Most teenagers do not kill themselves when their parents do something they do not like.

All suicides have multiple causes. There is no one event, be it a divorce, rage at a parent, or learning that one has a fatal illness, that leads directly to suicide. Those who do choose to commit suicide after any of these events are driven by other forces as well. *You did not cause the suicide of your loved one because there is never just one cause for suicide!*

The Real Muses of Suicide: Depression and Drugs

We are not going to attempt here, or anywhere else in this book, to offer a comprehensive review of why people do commit suicide. However, two major factors involved with suicide are serious depression and drug and alcohol abuse. No survivor can reasonably believe that he or she could have exerted control over a loved one's depression or addiction.

Both alcohol or drug dependence and serious depression can seriously impair a person's judgment. Alcohol and drug abuse also contribute to depression, since the "high" obtained from most substances is followed by a "crash," a bout of acute low feeling as the brain chemistry rebounds downward from the effects of the substance. A person in a serious depression, whether drug-induced or not, often feels profoundly hopeless and sees no prospect for life getting better. Individuals in such a frame of mind are prime candidates for suicidal impulses. They are also in the throes of a very powerful psychological, and at least partly biochemical, process—not something over which their loved ones have much control.

Codependence refers to the pattern of feeling and behavior that often develops in those involved in relationships with alcoholics and drug users. Just as the alcoholic is dependent on alcohol, and the addict is dependent on a drug, their families and loved ones ironically depend on the alcohol or drug: The quality of the families' lives depends on whether the substance abusers are using drugs and on how the drugs are affecting them. The more actively a person is using, the more severely her abuse is affecting her, and the more chaotic her family's life becomes.

We refer to the family members and loved ones who are thus at the mercy of the abuser's drug as being *codependents*. It is typical of codependent people to take on responsibility for the behavior of others, especially (but not only) the substance abuser whom they love. A codependent pattern assumed by many people

49

involved with alcoholics or drug users is to try to rescue their loved ones from their self-destructive addictions. They try all sorts of things to get their loved one to stop drinking or using drugs; they feel responsible if he does not quit. Sometimes they even believe that it is because of irritating traits in them that the person is a substance abuser.

It is only to be expected that when some of those alcoholic or drug-abusing individuals commit suicide, the codependent survivors will blame themselves. Having fallen into codependent patterns with their addicted loved ones, indeed having been almost irresistibly lured into codependence by the dynamics of addictive behavior, the survivors are set up for self-reproach and guilt.

If your loved one was alcoholic or drug dependent, it is likely that you acquired some codependent traits. If so, you were probably programmed to blame yourself for his behavior, and you felt guilty and responsible for his self-destructiveness. When he finally did kill himself, it was a virtual certainty that you would continue the same pattern of self-blaming. Now you probably feel the same guilt over his suicide that you previously felt over not getting him to quit his substance abuse.

Codependence is a complicated process. It is a very popular topic of many self-help books, which you may want to read. Some are listed in the Suggested Readings.

Al, the man who lived through his teenage and young adult years in terror that his alcoholic mother would succeed in killing herself, is a clear example of the codependent pattern. Al spent years believing that he would feel accountable for not "saving" her—*from herself*—if she did take her life.

If your loved one was alcoholic or drug dependent, at some point you may find it helpful to be part of an Al-Anon group, or some other support group for codependent people. (Alcoholics Anonymous and Al-Anon, the program for families of alcoholics, were really the forerunners of the self-help and support group movement, of which suicide survivor groups are just one example.)

The Final Verdict

Did *you have anything to do with your loved one's unhappiness? Possibly—but that's okay!* Most of you reading this book have tortured yourselves with the possibility that you could/should have done something differently, thereby preventing the suicide. By now, you know the answer: Yes, you could have done things differently, but you have no way of knowing if that would have prevented the suicide. Most of you yearn to conclude that there really was nothing that you could have done that would have made a difference. In order to believe that, you may rack yourself with an inquisition as to whether you did anything to contribute to your loved one's depression or unhappiness.

Although you feel so much guilt, and wish so much that you could escape it, the last thing you want to hear is that you probably did contribute to your loved one's unhappiness. But just about everyone in an intimate relationship does something, at some time, that makes the partner feel unhappy or angry or depressed or rejected. No one is a perfect lover or friend, parent or child. Only in one's wildest imagination, however, could that inevitable level of imperfection be equated with causing a person to take his or her life. Unfortunately, wild imagination is in ample supply among suicide survivors.

Chapter 13 is on healing. One part of healing from the trauma of a suicide is self-forgiveness. You need to accept that you might have done something differently, at some time, to have made the person you lost a little happier *without concluding that you are thus responsible for the suicide.* Part of your healing is understanding that just as suicide is a complex decision, so you are a complex person, with very ordinary and very human imperfections. If you feel guilt, you need to learn to forgive yourself.

It has been very easy while writing this chapter to mistype *blame* as *balm.* That unconscious slip is really a statement of the shift that needs to take place for you to heal: You need to stop blaming yourself, and to let understanding of both the suicide and of yourself be a balm for your emotional wounds.

Chapter 4

Shame

and Ostracism

In traditional Japanese society, the ritual suicide of *seppuku* (or *hara-kiri*) was not only acceptable behavior but was honorable and was even expected in some situations. Our society, and most contemporary societies, give suicide no such accepted, let alone honorable, place. Thus, suicide burdens people with shame. On top of all the grief, guilt, and anger that the survivors must endure, they often feel like outcasts, shamed in the eyes of their friends, neighbors, and co-workers.

In the history of our laws, specifically the common law of Great Britain, there was legally mandated "punishment" for suicide through desecration of the corpse. People who committed suicide were required to be buried at a crossroads, rather than in the church-consecrated grounds of a cemetery. British law required this until 1823, and until 1870 its penalty for suicide was thrust on the family of the dead person: All the suicide's property was forfeited to the Crown. Survivors were often left destitute. Even in the United States, suicide was technically illegal until the twentieth century.

In contemporary society, people do not publicly condemn suicide survivors, but they also do not know what to make of them. One of the surest ways to feel like an outcast is to know that you are being whispered about behind your back, and to sense glances directed at you when you aren't looking. Many members of our survivor groups have talked about being avoided by friends and neighbors after the suicide. Like Bill, in chapter 1, who experienced the discomfort of the people in his client's office when he said that his son had committed suicide, others have felt shunned rather than supported.

Emily found that mothers were reluctant to let the children who had once frequented her home play with her eleven-year-old daughter after the suicide of her teenage sister. Emily believed that the other mothers considered her to be unfit and not capable of supervising their children after her daughter's tragedy. When they didn't let their children come to play she thought that they believed she might contaminate their children in some way. Her observation that children were coming to play less frequently was accurate; her interpretation may not have been correct.

What is often happening when survivors encounter this avoidance is that people are so shocked (and, unconsciously, frightened) by a suicide that they have no idea what to say to the survivors. My friend Pete called me at my office one day, saying he needed some help urgently: His longtime colleague's son had just killed himself, and he was worried about what to say to her and how to deal with the situation. My friend is an intelligent and compassionate man, and one who is able to talk about feelings. He is not usually at a loss for words, but in this case he felt he needed help.

In fact, Pete had handled the situation very well. In his initial contact with his colleague Cynthia, after she got word of the suicide, he was very sensitive to her feelings. He talked openly with her about her son's long struggle with drugs, and he told her about the support group for suicide survivors that he knew I facilitated. On the phone with me not long afterward, he asked me what he could recommend for her to read and then went himself to buy her the book I recommended.

Despite all that, Pete had hurried to call me, worried that he might have said the wrong thing and unsure about what more to do. He and other colleagues were naturally inclined to travel to Cynthia's hometown for the funeral, but he wanted to make sure it was appropriate. I assured him that it was, and he went. But his self-doubt throughout this experience was truly striking.

Pete actually had handled the situation with Cynthia as sensitively as any survivor could hope for. He was willing to talk about the suicide, about her feelings, and about the struggles in her son's life. It was a natural impulse for him to want to go to the wake or funeral, and it was natural for him to feel uncertainty about going. He seemed to feel that the family might prefer to be alone, rather than having to face too many friends and colleagues at that difficult time. However, suicide survivors need and want support after the death. Fortunately, suicide is fairly rare. It is also very alien to most of us, not only because we are so seldom exposed to it but because the most basic human instinct is self-preservation.

This story about Pete is told to offer some sense of the confusion and uncertainty that even sensitive and aware people may feel when confronted with a suicide survivor. As the example of Pete clearly illustrates, a pulling back emotionally may not represent any condemnation or rejection of the survivor; a person may withdraw partly out of concern for making the survivor feel worse by intruding too much. All of that can be rooted in the instinctive dread that most people feel about suicide. Yet it is very easy for a vulnerable survivor to feel as though she is being shunned and treated as an outcast. Similarly the mothers who didn't permit frequent visits to Emily's home may have felt that they didn't want to burden Emily with extra children at a time that was difficult for her. Sensing the emotional fatigue that Emily was experiencing, they may have believed they were being considerate.

Even Helpers May Shun

At the beginning of this book, we mentioned that we had felt reluctance ourselves about trying to help suicide survivors face their feelings. Both of us initially felt that facilitating a suicide survivor group was not anything we were eager to do. We both knew we had this reaction to the idea, and yet we were not clearly aware of just why we felt this way.

After seriously exploring our own feelings, we have identified a number of specific factors that contributed to our reluctance. For one, after a suicide there has been a real trauma that cannot be undone, a terrible wound that a therapist (we feared) could do little to heal. We have since learned a good deal more about the healing power of the self-help group. We also anticipated (rightly) that there would be a good deal of hostility toward mental health professionals, since so many suicides represent failures of psychiatric treatment. This is certainly understandable, and it may well be that some suicide survivors would not want to come to a group facilitated by a mental health professional.

Despite such specific issues, we concluded that our initial reluctance to work with suicide survivors was not really based on these considerations but was more of a gut reaction—and a real shunning response. We felt an instinctive wish not to have to deal with the ominous forces that drive people to suicide. Admitting this to ourselves forced us to ask ourselves another question: Why should these forces bother us if we are talking about the survivors of suicide rather than suicidal individuals? In fact, we felt more wary of working with survivors than with suicidal people. Clearly this was not a rational response.

We concluded that we reacted with irrational fear of the darker side of human nature—*darker* because it seemed so foreign, so out of control, so deadly, even demonic. And we were struck by how we transferred our predictable, if irrational, dread of those forces from the person most afflicted by them (the one who had been driven to self-destruction) to those around him (the survivors).

We share this self-examination with you to give you a sense of the avoiding instincts triggered by suicide even in people who try to be in touch with their own feelings and who strive toward not condemning human frailties. Since we have worked with suicide survivors, we are no longer uncomfortable sharing our emotions; we have come to admire the courage, strength, and resiliency with which so many have endured this devastating trauma. Thus, it is all the more striking how reluctant we had initially been.

Others' Discomfort Becomes Your Rejection

Speaking about Pete and about our own reluctance to take on the task of facilitating survivor groups is meant to help you understand how other people may have their own instinctive fears that can cause them to avoid anything having to do with suicide, particularly survivors. They simply may have no idea what to say to you. For you, though, at a time when you are feeling your world has been turned upside down and you need all the help you can get to set it right again, such avoidance may make you feel like an outcast. You may already be feeling all sorts of guilt and a sense that your friends and neighbors are shunning you will fan the flames of your guilt into a raging sense of shame.

Shame is a particularly damning emotion. It is the escalation of guilt into an intense state of self-condemnation, which you believe is corroborated by your peers. So intense can shame be that it is next to impossible to step back from your situation and reevaluate yourself. This is why it is so important for you to know the experiences of other survivors, to know how common this feeling is among them. It is often much easier to listen to other survivors' stories, recognize that they are not guilty of the suicide, and they have no cause for shame. Perhaps as you exonerate others, you may begin to sense that you are not shameful either.

Exposing Secrets

We are social animals; we need the company of our fellow humans. We need approval of our peers—family, friends, neighbors, colleagues, and so on. Most of us do not "air our dirty laundry" in public. We would rather not reveal problems to outsiders, particularly problems that appear to reflect badly on us.

Suicide does not occur without there being problems. Happy, well-adjusted people do not kill themselves. (It is a complicated philosophical and ethical question whether there is such a thing as "rational" suicide in cases such as terminal illness. Even if there are "rational" suicides, however, they are a very small percentage of the total.)

In almost all cases, then, people who commit suicide are desperately unhappy. Most of the problems about which they are so unhappy—alcoholism, rejection in a relationship, the failure of a business—are issues that people generally try not to reveal to strangers. Sexual problems, overwhelming financial disasters, or other self-esteem–related matters are issues most families agree not to discuss with others.

The most pervasive contributing factor to suicide is profound depression. One part of such deep depressions is a sense of total despair, including the despair that no one else could ever understand what the depressed person is suffering. This leads to emotional isolation and a sense of futility about trying to communicate with anyone. It leaves one feeling different. It is true for the members of the family as well as for suicidal individuals.

Suicide reveals to the community that serious problems existed in the family that the family was unable to solve. Or so it seems to the survivors, who often feel that if they had been better able to deal with the problems, the suicide would not have occurred. Many families prefer not to reveal that death was caused by suicide in order to protect their own images. When such a fact is kept secret, feelings of shame fester. This perpetuates the denial that led to isolation in the first place. Secrecy precludes sharing, which can lead to the healing that comes with compassionate understanding.

Too often the fears or false sense of pride of one or two family members requires that others keep the secret. The more something is kept secret, the greater becomes its power to inflict feelings of shame and guilt. Often, once the hidden fact is revealed, you find that others already knew or suspected the truth. The truth helps everyone comprehend not only what has taken place but also others' reactions to it. The truth allows others to react in reassuring, comforting ways.

Let's consider some of the other factors often involved with suicide. As we have said earlier, drug and/or alcohol abuse is involved with at least half of the suicides that bring survivors to groups. Drug and alcohol abuse are highly socially stigmatized problems in our society, even though there is beginning to be more understanding of alcoholism and addiction as diseases, rather than as a moral weakness. Nonetheless, most people would be very reluctant to have an addiction problem in their families become widely known. A suicide by a drug- or alcohol-abusing individual becomes a doubly stigmatizing event if it reveals not only the suicide but the associated substance abuse problem.

Depression is what is most commonly associated with suicide. Depression, you might feel, is a more acceptable problem than alcoholism, for instance. But depression carries its own stigma. First, it is a kind of mental illness. Such problems are not as stigmatized as they used to be, and going to a psychotherapist is more acceptable, but the stigma is not entirely gone. Many people still feel some embarrassment about seeing a psychotherapist.

They often have a hard time telling friends or family they are doing so, and they are concerned that insurance claims for psychological treatment will become part of their permanent record. If one feels that much concern over seeing a therapist about "ordinary problems," serious depression must seem to be an unbearable embarrassment.

Depression makes people feel they have lost control and it makes them despair of anyone ever being able to help them, but it also makes them acutely sensitive to negative judgments. Despite how horribly they are suffering, depressed individuals are often very resistant to taking antidepressant medication because it implies they can't manage their own lives.

The final escalation of the shame occurs if hospitalization becomes necessary. Without question, there is stigma attached to being in a mental hospital. If, then, a suicide occurs after a period of depression, which may have included hospitalization, all the stigma that may be attached, or that families fear may be attached, to such treatment is added to the stigma of suicide.

Shame and the Media

Newspapers and the other media frequently augment the shame felt by a survivor when a suicide is made public with no sensitivity to what effect this reporting has on the survivors. For a survivor, a real person has died, not just someone whose life came to a tragic, if sensational, end. A survivor's shame can be magnified by tabloid papers combining grisly photographs of bodies with catchy headlines such as "Death Dive!" For survivors this sort of coverage is very painful. It is intrusive and disrespectful of people they loved who died in emotional pain. There is also shame when their loved ones' lives, as well as their deaths, are described in lurid fashion, when sensationalist media publish stories centering on sexual entanglements or drug involvement.

A survivor may find himself facing curious onlookers or spurious well-wishers prematurely when the suicide gets this kind of publicity. When a survivor's private problems enter the public domain he has to cope with shame with no opportunity to reflect on what the suicide means to him.

Less dramatic than such news accounts but not always less traumatic are the simple death notices or obituaries. Many people feel it is a violation of privacy when these report the death as a suicide. On the other hand, many families feel that it is helpful to their grieving to include the fact of the suicide in the death notice, in such a way as to show that suicide was only the end of the person's life and not the whole story. *A person's life should be remembered,* and not merely the manner in which he met his death. Suicide ends a life; it is not a description of that life. It is important that *how* a person lived her life be made known, not just the fact that she chose to end it.

The Power of the Unknown

Many suicide survivor support groups compile mailing lists including the names, addresses, and telephone numbers of all the people who attend the group regularly, and who they lost to suicide. As therapists, for whom confidentiality is a standard procedure, this practice at first seemed like a violation of confidentiality. But as the group facilitators explained, "We don't try to maintain confidentiality about the fact that we are suicide survivors because we don't think there's anything shameful about suicide, and we make that point by acknowledging openly that we are survivors."

Such openness does not come easily for all suicide survivors. Almost all the survivors we have talked with have avoided revealing how their loved one died, at least some of the time, and many deliberately misstate or avoid stating the cause of death. This is especially true when they are asked unexpectedly or are asked by someone with whom they are not particularly close, such as an acquaintance at a party saying, "Alex, I heard that Tom died.

I'm so sorry! What happened to him?" Survivors have talked repeatedly about how a chill can fall over a room, be it a social gathering or a business meeting, when they say that the death was a suicide.

Many survivors of suicide have explained the shocked and shunning reaction, as well as feelings of shame, that come from the revelation of suicide as the cause of a loved one's death. The feelings they describe are understandable, but they often involve *fear* of how people will respond more than specific thoughts of what those reactions will be. We believe that suicide is not something shameful to be kept as a guilty secret. However, since suicide can have a powerfully disturbing effect on others, and it may open up more about a survivor's life than he is prepared to reveal, when and how it is revealed should be the choice of the survivor.

Survivors dread the possibility of negative reactions, from shocked silence to grossly insensitive comments that actually have been said, for example, "What on earth had you done to him that he would kill himself?" In part, survivors sense that people will be at a loss as to how to deal with a suicide and will avoid them. But the fear of telling people about the suicide is more a belief that one just doesn't talk about things like that. Just as the act itself is taboo, so is talking about it.

Many survivors in our groups say, "Only here, with other survivors, can we readily talk about the details of how it happened. You have all been there too, and we know you will be able to accept our talking about it."

Secrets May Haunt You

Survivors may not feel ready to tell many people about the suicide. You may prefer to say that your husband had a heart attack, or that your daughter died in an accident. You insist that you simply are not ready to deal with people's reactions—and you are probably right; some of those reactions would be hard to deal with. The ultimate problem, though, about concealing the fact that your loved one's death was a suicide is the impact this has on you and your feelings. You are telling yourself, "This is something I need to keep hidden," which your emotions (if not your logical mind) will translate into, "This is something I have to be ashamed of."

Florence kept her husband's suicide a secret for many years. She rationalized her fear of revealing his suicide by believing that keeping it secret protected his memory. She thought that if people knew he had committed suicide they would think less of him. She was also afraid that they would think less of her and blame her in some way. Her children, mimicking her behavior, kept the secret too. All of them were afraid that others might shun them if the secret were known. Keeping the secret was not comfortable. It deprived them all of getting the comfort that sharing can bring. The longer the secret was kept, the more power it garnered to isolate them from having honest relationships.

Florence's children never told anyone at school that their father had taken his own life. Mother never actually told them that they shouldn't, but since she never shared the truth, they thought that they shouldn't either. They feared, because she did, that people would shun them if they knew.

Florence's daughter finally decided she would no longer keep the secret. It became too uncomfortable for her. She told her mother, "Once I knew that they knew, I didn't have to worry about them treating me like a weirdo if they found out." Florence learned a lot from her child.

Even when you believe that you have a very good reason for keeping a suicide a secret, you are probably creating more problems than you are solving. Richard's wife, like many who eventually take their own lives, had suffered from recurrent periods of extreme despondency. These episodes increased in severity and length after she developed heart problems. When she was in a despondent period, which was more and more of the time, she found it very hard to deal with her oldest son, David, especially after he turned thirteen and became a rebellious adolescent. Conflict was frequent. It seemed that everything David did upset his mother. "I can't take it anymore!" was her daily threat.

One day, when David ran from the house after a fight with her, she hung herself. Richard found her, and before David returned, her body had been removed from the house. Fearing that David would blame himself forever, Richard said that she had suffered from a sudden, fatal heart attack. How mother had died was a subject that father and son avoided for many years. David was sensitive to the fact that his father could not discuss his mother's death with him and he drew his own erroneous conclusions about why this was so.

The truth emerged only after David made a suicide attempt similar to his mother's, when he was eighteen. He said that he had always blamed himself for his mother's heart attack. He believed that the stress he caused by fighting with her had brought it on and the fact that his father could never discuss it with him convinced him that he was being blamed for her death. The distance between father and son that had come from keeping a painful secret had almost caused another tragedy. David's guilt led him to despise himself for having triggered his mother's heart attack.

When the facts emerged it became possible for father and son to build a trusting relationship, but there was much work that each of them needed to do. It was not until the suicide had been acknowledged that they could discuss the course of her life and come to an understanding that the intense conflict between mother and son was the result and not the cause of her depression. David's rebellion had been an understandable attempt to develop an independent existence, which was being thwarted by his mother's neediness. Perhaps if she had been less self-involved she could have been more sensitive to his adolescent strivings. David began to see that his behavior was not responsible for his mother's despondency—many other things were. Knowledge of the secret freed him and enabled him to be closer to the father whom he desperately needed.

The examples of Richard and David and the others cited in

this chapter illustrate that hiding feelings and keeping secrets almost never works well. When there are "unspeakable" elements of a family history or of personal feelings, malignant feelings and attitudes spread from concealment. The effects of obscuring and denying truth can be even worse than the feared reactions to revealing the truth.

Chapter 5

Ambivalence

Shakespeare's Marc Antony begins his eulogy of Julius Caesar with the words, "I come to bury Caesar, not to praise him. The evil that men do lives after them; the good is oft interred with their bones." Shakespeare really had this point wrong. We believe, "The good that men do is remembered after their deaths, and the evil tends to be forgotten." Most of us are not comfortable with angry or critical thoughts of the dead, especially those who have recently died.

If someone murdered a person we loved, we would be filled with rage toward the killer. We would hate him for taking the life of someone dear to us, and for all the pain that loss would cause us. In the case of a suicide, the killer and the victim are one and the same. This leaves many survivors in a state of intense ambivalence.

"I Loved Him . . . I Hated Him . . . I'm Glad He's Gone"

Most suicide survivors feel an uneasy blend of loving and angry feelings. The loving feelings are the natural grief for a loved one who has died. The hostile feelings involve anger at the person for causing so much pain by his suicide, anger at how he lived his life, and possibly even a sense of relief that a stormy, pain-filled life has ended. Whatever the specifics, the person who has committed suicide has caused you pain, and you feel angry at him for doing that.

Ambivalent feelings are almost universal after a suicide. There has usually been stress and conflict beforehand, and the pain caused by the suicide only creates more anger, which coexists with grief. Even when there has been little conflict with the person who killed himself, the suicide can cause anger because it seems to be such an outrageously hurtful and thus out-of-character act. Many survivors feel guilty about the hostile side of their ambivalence. It is important that they understand such feelings are universal and normal.

Idealizing the Lost Person

In the pain of losing a beloved friend or family member, most of us grieve over the good memories of that person. Our grieving is indeed the expression of our sense of loss. We are sad that happy times with him will not be repeated, and that happy oc-

66

casions we may have looked forward to will not come to pass. Hopes for the future are lost.

All of this is true in the case of deaths by suicide, too. We have a terrible sense of loss, and we think of all the loving feelings that can no longer be experienced, except in memory. After suicide, as after any death, there is often a wish to overlook the negative feelings, the unhappy memories of bad experiences, and to "let the bad be interred with the bones." The person who lives on in the memory of survivors is often an idealized figure, with all the blemishes removed.

When a person's memory is idealized after her death, it is difficult to let go of her and to let anyone else fill her place in your life, because no living person can possibly live up to the image you have created of the one who has died. After her sister Claudia committed suicide at the age of twenty-one, Sharon remembered that Claudia had not just been her sister but her best friend and the person whom she most admired in the world. She remembered Claudia as beautiful and bright and achieving and loved by everyone, and that she also sang in a haunting voice while accompanying herself on a guitar. Claudia was remembered as happy, cheerful, considerate of others, and forever smiling. In short, Claudia was remembered as one terrific person and as unlikely a candidate for suicide as you might expect to find. Sharon could find no way to even begin to understand what led to her sister's suicide, at least she couldn't as long as she continued to hold on to the belief that her sister had been a perfect person.

Because she could not or would not let herself remember what Claudia's real life was like, Sharon was left mystified, angry, and guilt ridden. If nothing in her sister's life could account for her death, then someone else—possibly Sharon herself—must be to blame.

After a few months of hearing about this perfect person, members of Sharon's support group began to tire of the litany of Claudia's unquestioned virtues. It was not that anyone thought that only bad or imperfect people commit suicide but rather that no one is ever without problems.

Eventually Sharon was able to dredge up some other memories of her sister. She recalled her dark, bitter, self-hating moods when she did not achieve her goals, for example, when someone else became the valedictorian of her college class. Claudia had raged that it was unfair and had refused to come out of her room for several days. Claudia seemed to need constant success and admiration. She could not share center stage with anyone; to maintain a good relationship with her you had to tacitly agree to remain in the background.

Once Sharon could admit that her sister had not been perfect, that sometimes she was angry at her or jealous of her, it became more possible for Sharon to truly mourn her loss. Now she was mourning for the real sister she had known and loved, but sometimes hated. None of us ever has feelings about another person that are always and only loving and positive: Conflicting feelings characterize the way we feel about almost everyone and everything.

Leila could not or would not remember one negative thing about her husband after his suicide. In fact, she flew into a rage if anyone suggested that her life with him had been difficult or unhappy in any way. Those who had known the couple described her husband Lou as being a self-centered, demanding man who depended on Leila to take care of him. He never had a job he was proud of, always believing that he was underpaid and undervalued. He frequently quit jobs before he had another one and let Leila support him and their children while he bemoaned his misfortunes. Leila now denied all of this, claiming that no one understood Lou. Whenever she felt a flash of anger at how Lou had lived and died, she quickly suppressed it by speaking of how wonderful he was.

Leila, like many others, was afraid to face her ambivalent feelings. By remembering only the good about Lou she could only blame herself for not taking good enough care of him. She took all the responsibility for his unhappiness and therefore for his suicide. When she did face his serious problems she stopped feeling completely responsible and was able to mourn his loss.

Margo idealized her son after he killed himself. She remembered only the most loving feelings. She missed him, was sad that his potential would never be realized, and was ashamed that she had been unable to make him want to live. She believed it was shame that made her angry at all the people who expressed sympathy, in whatever ways they could, for her loss. After almost a year had passed since his death, she found herself feeling angry and was about to make a snide, hostile comment to a well-wisher who was saying something comforting, when she had the sudden insight that it was not this person but her son with whom she was angry. It was he who had put her in this position, he who had created all this pain and grief and, in fact, it was he who had abandoned her by killing himself. She was not angry at her friends and family who were trying to support her through this troubled time; rather she was angry at her son who had made their comfort and pity necessary.

Relief

The Bells tried hard to be a perfect family. Rina and Mitch were a startlingly good-looking couple who lived a luxurious lifestyle. Their oldest daughter, Elaine, was an excellent student with many friends. She was the kind of child one could be proud of, and her parents saw her as living proof that they were successful in all ways.

This was not true of their younger son, Ted, who seemed to be out of step with the rest of the family from the day he was born. He was a colicky baby who never settled into a predictable sleep pattern, he became a whiny and quarrelsome toddler, and he was found to have severe learning problems when he entered school. By the time he was a teenager he was constantly in trouble and used drugs and alcohol extensively. Rina and Mitch battled with him, alternately indulging or punishing him, trying to get him to conform to the family standards in some way. Each was deeply and secretly ashamed of him and the heartache he created.

As much as Elaine's success confirmed them as good parents and people, Ted's difficulties destroyed their feelings of self-worth and challenged their decisions.

When he was twenty-two, Ted shot himself in the head. The Bells felt grief and horror at how he ended his life. They missed him very much. In the private recesses of their hearts they also felt relieved that he was dead and that they would no longer have to struggle with him, or worry about what kind of trouble he would get into next. They had always felt that in some ways he was not like them. His problems disrupted the way the rest of the family lived. While they felt genuine sorrow that he had taken his own life, they also felt angry that his suicide exposed them as a troubled family, just as his behavior had when he was alive.

"I Hate You for Doing This to Me!"

This is not exactly a loving comment, but it is one that erupts from many survivors. Many survivors are angered at the pain inflicted on them by the person who has committed suicide. Many are especially enraged by their certainty that the one who took his own life *wanted* to cause them pain. Spouses are particularly prone to this sort of rage. Husbands and wives, or lovers, make intense emotional demands on each other and may threaten suicide if those needs are not met. Some use threats to hold a partner in a relationship. When a suicide occurs after such threats, a survivor can feel very strongly that it was in retaliation, which leaves a dual legacy of guilt and rage.

We remind you again that there is never just one cause for a suicide. Despite what the person may have threatened, no one kills himself or herself *only* because a spouse or lover is not loving or caring enough. The overwhelming majority of spouses with grievances against their mates do not commit suicide. If one's spouse is really not meeting his needs, or if a couple simply cannot get along, separation or divorce is a better option than suicide. Those who choose suicide are driven by other dark forces within themselves.

Phyllis had been married to her husband, Ed, for over twenty years, and though it was not a perfect marriage, there had always been a great deal of closeness between them. The younger two of their four children were in their teens. Phyllis knew that she would feel the loss when these kids went off to college, but she had also looked forward to having Ed all to herself again. She hoped for a renewal of their former romance.

When the youngest, Janice, was in her midteens, Ed became depressed, partly in reaction to the failure of his business. He began to drink heavily. He was moody and increasingly angry when he was drunk. Things reached crisis proportions when Ed started to come home drunk every day. He humiliated the kids in front of their friends and was having alcoholic blackouts. The next day he would have absolutely no recollection of what he had done.

At that point, Phyllis decided to move out, rather than subjecting both the kids and herself to Ed's drunken behavior. She took her daughter and moved to her parents' home. When she did, some of the old Ed emerged from his alcoholic haze: He expressed remorse over his drinking and his embarrassing behavior toward the family and vowed to straighten himself out. He began by attending AA meetings. Fortunately, Phyllis had gone to Al-Anon, and sought counseling for herself. She knew that relapses are not uncommon in early recovery, and that just because Ed began treatment, there was no guarantee that his drinking problem was under control.

Very soon Ed stopped going to AA and resumed drinking. He became even more angry. He frequently telephoned Phyllis and complained about how "life has screwed me." His moods fluctuated between this foul temper and more rational moments when he pleaded with Phyllis to come back to him. In the angry moods he threatened her with a bitter divorce contest if she did not return. He then even began to escalate his threats to include committing suicide. Phyllis was frantic over these threats but self-protective enough to realize how unhealthy it would be if she were to return to Ed under duress of threats.

After one such phone call, Ed shot himself. He left a note saying he couldn't go on living without his children, with the implication that Phyllis had cut him off from them. Naturally, Phyllis felt a lot of guilt, going through the usual litany of "I should have . . ." and "If only I had. . . ." Even while she was doing that, Phyllis realized she felt enraged at Ed. She was quite certain—and it seemed a reasonable conclusion, based on what he had said to her—that he wanted to hurt her, to make her feel guilty that she had not given in to his demands. She also felt a real sense of loss, not for the Ed she had known during the recent months but for the Ed she had loved for many years.

The ambivalence Phyllis experienced is the clearest kind of ambivalence suicide survivors face: simultaneous hatred for the person who wanted to hurt them and grief for the person they loved so much. Another form of ambivalence is a mixture of grief and relief that the person has died.

"At Least We Don't Worry About Him Anymore"

Dave was a young man who experienced a very stormy adolescence. By the time he reached his eighteenth birthday, he was abusing both alcohol and cocaine, and had had two accidents while driving under the influence of alcohol. In one of these accidents, a passenger in the car Dave hit had been seriously injured, and her life had been in serious danger for several days afterward. In between his periods of wildness, Dave was often deeply depressed: He felt that his life was going nowhere, and he felt abandoned by his girlfriend, who finally broke up with him over his drinking and drugging. During one of these depressions, Dave used the exhaust from his car to asphyxiate himself.

Dave's father, Phil, had tried to help him, urging him to go to therapy, and going to family counseling sessions with him. When Dave killed himself, Phil was plunged into the agonized grief of all parent-survivors. At the same time, he felt that a huge amount of tension had finally been drained out of his life, and he experienced a deep sense of relief.

At first, when Phil had some momentary awareness of this relief, he felt terribly guilty and tried desperately to avoid these feelings. Finally he couldn't ignore them any longer. Phil recognized that he was feeling relieved. He no longer had to worry about the consequences of Dave's behavior, and he was relieved from the burden of trying to rescue Dave from his problems.

The first set of relieved feelings, of not having to worry about the consequences of Dave's behavior, was a little easier for Phil to face. He remembered all the times Dave had been out late, most likely drinking with his friends. Phil used to live in dread of a phone call bringing dire news. His worst fears had been realized some months earlier when he got a call from a state trooper telling him of Dave's car accident. Although Phil had quickly been reassured that his son's injuries were not life-threatening, he suffered through several nightmarish days while the passenger in the other car remained in critical condition. On top of all Dave's other problems, Phil faced the horror of his son being responsible for the death of an innocent person.

Even after the accident, Dave still drank and drugged; he denied that his intoxication had caused the accident, blaming it on the slippery road. With good reason, Phil had awaited another phone call with dreadful news. It had gotten so bad that once, when the phone rang close to midnight, he broke into a sweat. Since Dave's death, Phil was relieved of that dread. In fact, it was the ring of the telephone one evening that made Phil aware of his feelings: He had a momentary panic feeling, then caught himself relaxing, realizing he didn't need to worry anymore about what Dave had done. At first he felt guilty that he could let himself find anything positive about Dave's death, but he was able to realize he was simply being realistic.

No More Rescue Attempts

Phil was also relieved to be free from the impossible burden of trying to rescue Dave from his alcohol and drug dependence. (Many survivors may identify with this part of Phil's story, since so many suicides involve drug or alcohol abuse.) Like most family members of substance abusers—especially parents of substance abusers—Phil had tried to change Dave's drinking and drugging behavior. Phil had taken the initiative to get counseling for Dave and the family. He had tried to regulate his son's behavior to keep him away from the people and places associated with drinking and drugging. He had also tried to figure out what he might have done wrong in raising Dave that could have led to the substance abuse.

Phil found out that no one can be responsible for someone else's behavior. While learning this, the families are burdened with chronic guilt and anxiety. After Dave's suicide, Phil no longer had to feel responsible for trying to stop his substance abuse. The relief was hard for him to accept, since it stirred up doubts about whether he could have done more for Dave. With the help of his support group, Phil was able to see that it was never possible for him to do more to help his son. Now he owed it to himself to enjoy the relief from trying to struggle with that problem.

Frequently, relief at a death exposes previously hidden anger. In Phil's case, his relief from trying to rescue Dave made him aware of the anger he had suppressed over the years at his son's irresponsible behavior, the pain it caused his parents, and the harm he did to other people. At first, Phil felt guilty about this anger, too, but his group helped him recognize that it was justified by Dave's behavior.

Most people who kill themselves have been very unhappy for a long time, and very unhappy people are often difficult to live with. Depression is certainly the most common precursor of suicide, and many people have endured years of depression before finally ending their lives. Depressed people are not enjoyable companions. Indeed, those close to depressed people, if they are truly empathic, often come to share the depressed person's sense of hopelessness about himself and his belief that all efforts to help him will be futile. Consequently, they often feel very frustrated and exhausted by their efforts to help.

If a depressed person has threatened suicide repeatedly, those close to her may find themselves occasionally thinking, "Just go ahead and do it, get it over with, and stop torturing us this way!" Such feelings usually cause great guilt in the person who has them, and they constitute a particularly strong foundation for ambivalence after a suicide.

Chapter 6

ᘓᘓ

Depression

Pervasive sadness, a sense that life is without meaning or joy, a persistent lump in the throat or a feeling that tears are imminent—most of us would call this depression. Mornings when it is particularly hard to get out of bed, nights when sleep won't come, and times when none of the usual pleasures of life are appealing are familiar aspects of depression and all are to some degree part of life.

For some, these unhappy episodes pass before they are really noticed. For others they take hold, deepen, and begin to darken every waking and sleepless moment. Unhappiness becomes constant gloom, anxiety turns to dread, insomnia robs one of healing sleep, loss of appetite leads to weight loss and withdrawal. Life feels like an unwanted burden.

Depression can be only one of many moods or it can become a predominant theme, eclipsing other feelings. It can be a normal experience or it can become a life-threatening illness. It is the most pervasive theme of suicide and suicide survivors. That someone would want to escape from life is indicative of severe depression. Survivors, weighed down by their grief, certainly *feel* depressed. What is depression, though? Are survivors depressed in the pathological sense? Or are they only experiencing normal mourning reactions? These are the first questions we need to address.

What Is Depression?

Depression is not a strictly pathological state of mind. All of us, in the normal course of events, have times when we feel down or blue. This is most natural when we are reacting to something bad that has happened, such as failing a course in school or not getting a promotion we had hoped for or fighting with a friend. When things like this happen it is perfectly natural to say, "I'm feeling depressed today."

Much more intense depression may also be natural and normal. The most common cause for serious but normal depression is a significant loss. Losses that may precipitate a serious depression include divorce, job loss, and physical illness. The death of a loved one causes almost everyone to become depressed.

Normal Grief in Mourning

Some of the things you may feel that are associated with "normal" grief after the death of a loved one are: feeling physically unwell, preoccupation with thoughts of the deceased, guilt feelings in which you accuse yourself of negligence, hostility toward doctors and others, and changes in everyday behavior, such as restlessness or lethargy, inability to organize activities or to carry on ordinary socializing. Suicide survivors will find all of these problems very familiar.

Certainly everyone who has just lost a loved one feels very sad. No joy is found in life. Appetites for both food and sexual pleasure fade, creating a state called *anhedonia,* or a lack of pleasure-seeking. Even sleep and the escape it gives from the stresses of waking hours may become elusive. People experiencing intense grief may find it difficult to fall asleep, and they may wake up in the early-morning hours and find it difficult to get back to sleep. In the immediate aftermath of the death of someone close—and not just by suicide—survivors may feel that life will never be joyful again. There can be other manifestations of depression that may not be recognized so readily. These include irritability, lethargy (especially finding it very difficult to get out of bed in the morning), forgetfulness, and neglect of one's appearance or health.

Clinical Depression

All of the symptoms just described are also considered signs of clinical depression, that is, a depression regarded as a psychological disorder and not just an everyday part of life. If the symptoms last no more than four to six weeks, and then gradually abate, they constitute normal grieving, despite their mimicking of clinical depression. When they persist for longer than six weeks, as they do for many suicide survivors, clinical depression is the diagnosis.

What usually helps mourners to recover from their grief are the cultural rituals that surround mourning. Most commonly the rituals of mourning include reminiscing about the deceased loved one, sharing grief with family and friends, and supportive reassurances of others close to you who have experienced the same thing. You are supported by hearing that your unhappiness is natural and will pass as time goes by.

It is not surprising that the grief of many suicide survivors does not abate as readily as that of some other mourners, since suicide survivors are deprived of many of the comforting and reassuring aspects of the mourning process. Many suicide survivors feel stigmatized and ostracized and are the recipients of implicit or explicit messages that they should not talk about the suicide. Perhaps much more often than not, there is no reference to the death being a suicide during the funeral rituals. This is a function both of the stigma and of the fact that those who have never experienced a suicide are often at a total loss as to how to talk about it. Whatever the reasons, a veil of silence is often draped over the suicide. Many survivors contribute unwittingly to this silence when, in their initial, horrified reaction to the suicide, they conceal the cause of the death.

When sharing is not allowed to happen, mourning is impeded. The suicide survivors go through self-blame and cannot speak openly about the event and the guilt they feel. When they do not speak, no one can provide reassurance. This inability to seek and receive reassurance contributes to clinical depression in the survivors.

Patterns of Depression

Suicide survivors must understand what depression is and how it can be treated. It is important to recognize when the expectable, normal grief of mourning has turned into depression, so that you will know when professional help is needed.

Depression can often be a familial pattern, that is, it occurs much more commonly in some families than in others. Not everyone in these families will become depressed, but people in these families have a higher than average probability of becoming depressed, especially when coping with difficult situations. Thus, blood relatives of a person who had been seriously depressed before committing suicide may also be predisposed to depression. Suffering a traumatic loss like the suicide of a family member can be a powerful trigger. Thus, all suicide survivors are at risk for depression. It is important for them and those who are involved with them to recognize the signs of depression and to know what treatment is available.

Wanting to die is a strong indicator of a depressed state of mind. Almost everyone who commits suicide has been seriously depressed. It would be remarkable for someone who was not depressed to choose to end his life, though there could be uncommon factors operating that might lead a nondepressed person to suicide. These include a person being thoroughly disoriented in his thinking due to intoxication with such drugs as LSD or PCP ("angel dust"), or a schizophrenic individual hearing voices telling him to kill himself because of his sins.

Since depression and hopelessness are such pervasive themes for people who take their own lives, having some understanding of depression may help suicide survivors answer the questions, "Why did she do it? What could make her want to kill herself?"

Many authors have eloquently described the depressive experience. Perhaps it has been described most poignantly by William Styron in his autobiographical work *Darkness Visible*. He painfully describes his own depression, which almost led him to suicide. His recognition of how close to death he was and his request for psychiatric hospitalization saved his life.

Types of
Depressive Disorders

The mental health profession considers depressive disorders to be disturbances of mood. The term *mood disorder* refers to a disturbance that shifts the individual's usual moods out of the normal range, beyond the everyday upward and downward swings. The intense depression occurring in the immediate aftermath of the death of a loved one is considered part of the normal grieving process, and thus would not be considered a pathological mood disturbance.

Mood disorders are divided into two categories: bipolar disorders and depressive disorders. The term *bipolar* has replaced *manic depressive*. It refers to disorders in which there are mood swings in two directions: downward into depression and upward into mania, which is a state of exaggerated good mood, characterized by elation, rapid speech, wildly optimistic thinking, high levels of physical energy and activity, and decreased need for sleep. The various types of bipolar disorders are defined by the severity of both the depressive and the manic episodes, and according to whether the disorder is cyclic (that is, alternating between the depressive and the manic), or predominantly of one type or the other. We will not elaborate further on bipolar disorders here, since it is depression that interests us. Suffice it to say that the types of depressive disorders we will discuss could constitute part of a bipolar disorder if there are concomitant manic episodes.

Depressive disorders run the gamut from very severe, incapacitating depressions in which virtually all aspects of a person's functioning are disturbed to depressions that merely leave one feeling "blue" or unhappy. Some depressions occur as a response to a clearly identifiable life stressor: the loss of a loved one, the loss of a job, the illness of a child. You can surely think of other situations that could cause unhappiness. When the stimulus for a depressed response is easy to recognize, even a strong depressed reaction is understandable. If the depressed feelings do not last very long and are not disruptive to a person's life, there is usually no great cause for alarm.

Sometimes, however, depressions occur for no apparent reason. If the depression appears to be more than just "blue" feelings, and if it includes disturbances in sleeping or eating, feelings of slowness or sluggishness, or withdrawal from usual social contacts or daily routine, seeking professional help is necessary.

Depression and Suicide

Suicidal thoughts or impulses are almost always indicators of serious depression. Serious depression always raises the *risk* of suicidal thoughts or impulses. This is not to say that everyone who is depressed is suicidal. The risk of suicide must always be part of a clinician's assessment of a depressive disorder. When there are some suicidal thoughts or urges present, that becomes a major consideration in determining the appropriate treatment.

When there are signs of suicide, managing this danger becomes the primary focus of intervention. Hospitalization is often indicated because it is the surest and quickest means of protecting the person from acting on suicidal impulses. However, hospitalization is no guarantee against a person committing suicide.

Suicidal Urges
in Suicide Survivors

Many survivors worry that they or their family members are now more at risk for suicidal behavior. They have heard that suicide survivors are more likely to commit suicide than others. This fear turns out to be statistically true, though the reasons for it are not totally clear. It is primarily because depression runs in families, and families with more depression are more likely to have had someone who committed suicide than families with no pattern of depression. Thus, it is particularly important for survivors to seek treatment if they become depressed.

A number of survivors in our groups have histories of suicide attempts, but they have obtained treatment. That they are no longer feeling suicidal is evidence that suicidal depression can be overcome. This is important, since many survivors have lost faith in mental health professionals, whom they see as having "failed" when their loved ones took their own lives.

Treatments for Depression

There are two main forms of treatment for depression: psycho-therapy and antidepressant medication. A third treatment, electric shock, also called electroconvulsive therapy (ECT), is used with particularly severe depressions, especially when they do not re-spond to medication, but this is done with a small percentage of depressed patients.

There are a number of antidepressant medications available today. Different types seem to work better with different types of depression. A psychiatrist, who is a medical doctor, is the person to consult about whether you could benefit from antidepressant medication and which type would be best for you.

Antidepressants are not a "quick fix." Taking them is not like taking an aspirin to cure a headache. None of them provide im-mediate relief. They generally take at least two weeks before you can expect to feel a significant lessening of depression. Prozac, which is now the most widely used antidepressant, can take as long as six weeks to develop its maximum effectiveness. It is important to be aware of this and not to become discouraged if you do not feel better after taking an antidepressant for a week or so. You may feel like stopping the medication in the mistaken belief that it is not helping. If an antidepressant is prescribed for you, it is important that you give it time to work. Also, even if one antidepressant fails to help much, another may work much better for you.

Is Depression
Physical or Psychological?

This extremely complex and much debated question is beyond the scope of this book. We believe that *both* emotional-psycho-logical and physiological-hereditary factors can cause depression and that in many people who are depressed both are contributing factors. Those who believe depression is almost entirely physiological in origin will lean toward physical treatment—generally medication. People who emphasize the cognitive and emotional causes of depression will lean toward psychotherapy as the treatment of choice. We feel, as do most clinicians these days, that both medication and psychotherapy can be effective in treating depression. Some people will do better with medication, others with therapy, and many benefit from a combination of the two.

Depression tends to perpetuate itself. Once you are feeling depressed, you will tend to see everything through the eyes of depression. You will most readily focus on the possible negative outcomes of your choices and feel pessimistic about the future. You will find it very hard to have confidence in the ability of anyone or anything to help you feel less depressed. Even a depressed state that may have been triggered by some physiological factor creates a depressed outlook on life. Once you are in a depressive mode, positive outcomes become difficult to see.

Antidepressant medications can begin to break a physiologic depressive slide. They may even help to prevent a recurrence in those whose depressions occur in cycles. Psychotherapy also can help alleviate depression. "Cognitive therapy" helps people learn how to replace their self-defeating thoughts with more realistic ones, thereby breaking the pattern of always seeing things negatively. Behavior therapy seeks to change specific symptoms or problems that may be contributing to the depression. The psychodynamic approach uncovers internal emotional conflicts and feelings which may be repressed. By coming to terms with resentments, conflicts, and fears, the depression these have caused gradually dissipates. In sum, different therapeutic approaches are better for dealing with different types of depressions.

Understanding the Suicide

What you have read is that there are a variety of depressive disorders and a variety of treatments for them. No one treatment can be guaranteed to be best for an individual. This is a very important point for survivors, who repeatedly blame themselves for not having recognized their loved one's depression and for not getting treatment that would have prevented the suicide. It is unrealistic for survivors to blame themselves for that failure, when even highly trained professionals must sometimes rely on trial and error to see which treatment works best for a particular patient.

Even hospitalization is not a certain intervention. A hospital cannot absolutely prevent a suicide if a person is determined to do it. Patients have found ways to kill themselves even while under observation in locked psychiatric wards. The transition out of the hospital, occurring when the depression is lessening but is probably not totally overcome, can also be a dangerous time.

The stress of leaving the protected environment of the hospital and returning to the burdens and challenges of everyday life can be difficult to handle.

For many people who experience major depressive episodes *the risk of suicide is greatest when they are beginning to feel better*. When people are in the depths of a major depression they may lack the energy to commit suicide. Ironically, when they begin to experience some alleviation of the depression, they may regain some energy while still sufficiently depressed. It is at this point that they may be most likely to attempt suicide.

Some patients are so determined to attempt suicide that they may deliberately mislead doctors or hospital staff. "Don't think that we don't know just how to manipulate the hospitals," explained a formerly suicidal man whose friend had just killed himself while on a pass from a psychiatric hospital. "When we want to be confined in a hospital we tell them that we are suicidal; when we want to get out we insist that we aren't. My friend had decided the time had come and so he asked for a pass, denied that he was having suicidal thoughts, and went out and blew his brains out."

Thus, even for very capable professionals, assessing suicidal risk and preventing suicidal acts when the risk is recognized are not certain things. If highly trained professionals cannot be absolutely sure, then families should not believe they might have been able to prevent the suicide.

Chapter 7

Pitfalls of the Healing Process

Healing after the suicide of a loved one is a lengthy process for most people. Typically a survivor moves from hopelessness and despair to recovery and resolution. However, you may suddenly find yourself back where you started. We have found that there are predictable circumstances that may trigger feelings the survivor believed had already been put to rest. In this chapter we help you prepare for these experiences, making them easier to handle when they arise. We also alert you to other difficulties you may encounter during the healing process.

Anniversary Reactions

The yearly, monthly, or even weekly anniversary of the death is a frequent stimulus for depression and despair. Feelings at these times can be as intense as the reactions of the earliest days. When you examine the times at which your own depressions recur with the greatest intensity you are likely to discover some pattern related to an anniversary. If this is true, you will be able to predict and prepare for bouts of unhappiness.

Suicide anniversaries stimulate painful awareness of the absence of your loved one. Your sense of loss is accentuated by that person not being there to do certain things and react in certain ways. We have found the adage, "Forewarned is forearmed," to be true for anniversary reactions. You will find that changing routines will help diminish the pain you feel.

Bob knew he had an anniversary reaction every Sunday. It was the last day he had spent with his wife before she committed suicide. He found that Sunday was the worst day of his week. She was no longer there for their walk to buy the newspaper or to argue over who was going to have first crack at the crossword puzzle. She no longer ironed their clothing for the coming week while he watched sports on T.V. They had spent Sunday at home getting ready for the work week.

Bob found he had to change his Sunday routine so he would be less aware of his wife's absence. He made sure he was out of the house for most of the day. He did not stop missing his wife, but he was able to alleviate the weekly trauma and sadness of a day at home.

Julia found she could not leave the house on Thursday because she found her daughter's body hanging in the basement on a Thursday. She believed that if she had not left her house that fateful day the suicide would not have occurred. She now felt that if she remained at home on Thursday nothing else bad could ever happen. Gradually she let go of her fear of Thursday, but she shifted her anxiety to the seventeenth of every month, the date on which the suicide occurred. Still later, she could get past that day of the month, but she never forgot the yearly anniversary of her daughter's death. She learned to anticipate and make plans for that day.

Earl's twenty-five-year-old son committed suicide two years ago. Earl felt he had been making a satisfactory recovery. He was living with much of the zest he had before. Although his wife still attended a support group, he had stopped doing so when another activity he enjoyed was scheduled at the same time. Together they had begun to prepare for the first Thanksgiving they were willing to have at home since their son's death. Thanksgiving had always been a special family holiday. Earl and his eldest son had a tradition of spit-roasting the turkey on a fire in the backyard. On the day after Thanksgiving they had always gone to a farm in the country to cut the family's Christmas tree.

As the time approached, Earl did not want to tell his wife that he felt increasingly less and less enthusiastic about the holiday plans. In fact, he was secretly dreading Thanksgiving. He had disturbing dreams. He would awaken at 4:00 A.M. to wander apprehensively through his dark house. He began spending more time alone, unwilling to participate in his once active social life. A professional clinician might have said that he was depressed. Neither Earl nor his wife could understand what was going on. What was causing him to be so upset right now?

Not knowing what else to do, Earl's wife got him to come to a support group meeting. As he began to talk he realized that Thanksgiving was the last time he and his son had had a good time together before the final decline that led to his suicide at the end of December. Although the recognition that his depression was an anniversary reaction did not make his gloomy feelings disappear, it did make his dark mood more understandable. He felt less out of control.

Earl decided to go ahead with the Thanksgiving celebration but not to repeat some of the traditions, especially those with which his son had been most involved. He would not spit-roast the turkey. He and his wife planned ways to remember their son at this special time. Earl prepared a short statement about his son to read at the family gathering. The preparation process was helpful to him as he reminisced about happy times with his son.

An anniversary is a time to remember. Rather than hoping that each succeeding anniversary will bring less painful remembrances than the one before, you can plan how you wish to remember your loved one. When you plan a time for remembering, for reminiscing about past events, for sharing a song, poem, or reading that evokes a special memory, you celebrate the person you have lost.

Jason's family played a recording of Bach's "Cantata and Fugue in C" every year when they gathered on the anniversary of his suicide. It was his favorite piece of music and it evoked memories of Jason sitting on the family deck enjoying the outdoors while he listened to his stereo. Florence's family liked to meet at a different restaurant on each anniversary of her suicide. Whereas other families might consider this frivolous, her family was celebrating her passion for trying out new places to eat. Another brother and sister remembered the anniversary of their mother's suicide every year by going someplace that she had never been but had wanted to go. They would talk about how much she would have enjoyed the excursion. They found that this was a perfect way to reminisce, while affirming that life is for the living and must continue.

The Importance of Rituals

Most religions, recognizing the universality of anniversary reactions to death, provide rituals for remembrance. Catholics remember anniversaries by having masses said in honor of the deceased. Jewish families light candles in the home and say a special prayer of remembrance in the synagogue. At public gatherings it is traditional to remember someone with a moment of silence. Graves and memorial sites are visited on significant days to preserve the memories of loved ones. The ritualization of remembering provides a time and method for thinking about the deceased.

Rituals are an acknowledgment that we all have a need to think about those we have lost. By providing specific times and ways of doing so, rituals can also free us to think about other things at other times.

Julia, who did not adhere to any religious practice, found that she had to create her own ritual for the anniversary of her daughter's suicide. She chose to spend part of the day alone looking over photographs of her daughter's life. This was a time of intense remembrance for her. Later she would have her other children and their families for dinner and together they would remember their dead sister. This became an important time in all their lives. While it allowed them all to remember, it also freed them to forget, or at least to not be involved in constant rumination about the suicide at other times. A time, a place, and a method for remembering had been created.

Milestones as Emotional Triggers

Normal changes that occur may also seem to reverse the progress being made toward recovery. Change is associated with growth but also with loss. Graduations, weddings, movies, even promotions mean moving on to something new while giving up something of the past. Each new step in your life moves you away from the experiences you shared with the deceased. At these times the deceased's presence may be sharply missed, even after feelings of loss are no longer a part of daily life.

When Donna's husband, an aspiring actor, received his first favorable review in a well-known newspaper she was ecstatic for a few hours. Suddenly she felt herself plunge into despair as she realized her sister, who had committed suicide only three months before, would never be able to share their joy. That night when her husband wanted to celebrate his good news she became enraged at him. She felt guilty that she and her husband were moving on to better times and leaving her sister behind.

Donna wrote a letter to her dead sister telling her everything that she was feeling. She even told her how angry she was at her for giving up. Her suicide frightened Donna, who herself had entertained suicidal thoughts during some of her own difficult times. Writing this letter was comforting for Donna because it made her feel as if she were still in touch with her sister, even though she was painfully aware that her sister would never read it. Through the writing she was able to clarify her own confused thoughts and focus more on what was happening in her life. Donna continued to make good use of letter writing to "communicate" with her sister for many years. It was her private way of keeping her sister with her in spirit whenever she wanted her to be there.

Pretending That Nothing Else Matters

The loss of a loved one through suicide is probably the worst thing that will ever happen to you. It puts other problems into a different perspective for most survivors. However, as painful as the suicide of a loved one is, it is not the only difficulty that most of us face. One danger during recovery can be blaming all unhappiness on the suicide. You may feel as if nothing else matters. It becomes a convenient excuse for not having to deal with other problems. Although we would never place a time limit on how long your mourning should continue, we also urge survivors to be aware that there may be other things bothering them. Other problems must be faced.

A hint that you may be using your pain over the suicide to hide from other problems is if your feelings remain fixed and unchanged for a long period of time. Grieving is a process that ebbs and flows. Even the most deeply bereaved mourners have feelings that move to hopefulness and relief some of the time. It is normal for the human spirit to wish to overcome and survive the darkest tragedy. If you remain mired in unchanging gloom, with no relief, you may be using your reaction to this tragedy to avoid confronting other things that may be troubling you.

Jim's marriage had been troubled for many years, even before his son committed suicide. Jim and his wife had always been so involved with their son's recurrent depressions and the problems these created that they had been able to avoid dealing with their marital problems. Now that Paul was dead, his suicide provided a new way for them to avoid each other. Jim seemed stuck in his mourning for his dead son in an unremitting and unchanging way.

Jim attended every meeting of a support group, but nothing seemed to help him move beyond a ritualized retelling of the story of his son's death and how it had ruined his life forever. He found no satisfaction in anything else in his life, including the love of his other children. In Jim's case, being upset for a long time was not an indicator that something else might be wrong, since many people stay upset for a long time. It was that his upset was always the same. Whenever anyone suggested that he might look at other things in his life he would become angry and respond that his son's suicide had made everything else irrelevant.

Jim's marital problems became worse. He dismissed his wife's complaints with a passive attitude of "What can you expect from me—my son committed suicide." It was not until his wife threatened to divorce him and took steps to move out—facing Jim with another significant loss in his life—that he became more willing to face these problems. Jim and his wife began marital counseling. There were no magical solutions for them, but once they began facing some of their problems they did begin to find some answers. Their son's suicide will always be with them as a painful part of their lives. They cannot change it, but now they no longer use it to mask other painful problems that can be worked out.

Thinking
About Suicide Yourself

One of the most frightening reactions you may have to the suicide of a loved one is wishing to take your own life. For some of you this feeling may come right after the discovery of the suicide. It is a response to the intense pain and grief that you feel. Almost all of the survivors that we have met report having had fleeting thoughts that their own suicide would be a way of escaping from these feelings. Thoughts of suicide may recur for some time as the reality of what has happened becomes real to you. We strongly urge all survivors to remove weapons or other means of self-destruction from their homes.

An even more frightening impulse overtakes many survivors in the ensuing months as they struggle to truly understand the final acts of their loved ones. It is a statistical observation that once a suicide has occurred in a family, its members are at greater risk for suicidal behavior. We are not sure why this is so. It may have something to do with inherited biochemical structures. It may be related to the repetition of learned behaviors. Whatever the reason, be alert to this risk. Rid yourselves of self-destructive tools, especially those that the deceased used.

Jason loved his son and mourned intensely for a long time after he jumped from the roof of a fourteen-story building. He was particularly preoccupied, as many survivors are, with trying to comprehend this seemingly insane act. Thoughts about the suicide were seldom out of his mind as he examined the possible scenarios that might have led to that fatal leap. He found himself staring out of windows and leaning over the edges of balconies wondering what his son had experienced. Though he often felt despondent, he could not believe what his son had done.

One evening, Jason was alone at work on a high floor of his office building. Pausing from the work, he began thinking about his lost son. He felt as if he were being inexplicably drawn to the windows. He reports that it was difficult to resist the urge to step out of the window to his death. He was so frightened by this strange compulsion that he made sure he was never alone in the office again.

Ruth, whose daughter shot herself, was similarly obsessed with trying to figure out why. She frequently retraced the steps her daughter must have taken on the morning that she shot herself in her bathroom. She would stand by the bathroom sink, staring at her own reflection in the mirror, trying to get inside of her daughter's head. She would then climb the attic stairs, as her daughter must have done, and would reach into the old trunk in which the gun was kept. She would return to the bathroom mirror and think some more. One day she varied the routine by actually retrieving the gun, which had been returned to the same trunk where it previously was kept. This time when she returned to the bathroom she put the gun to her temple, just the way her daughter had done. She has never been able to explain why she did not complete the act as her daughter had. She was sufficiently scared by her actions to give away the gun so she would never be tempted to repeat that sequence of events.

Substance Abuse

Looking at pain, feeling it, examining it, finding its roots and, most of all, not hiding from it are what we believe bring about growth and healing. One of the most common ways of masking pain and preventing recovery is through substance abuse. We have found that many survivors increase their use of alcohol or drugs during the aftermath of a suicide. We urge you not to take this route to pain reduction. Although you may experience an initial dulling of bad feelings, you are merely postponing facing the pain that loss brings.

Chemical dependency and substance abuse are known factors in a large number of suicides. Many people who commit suicide first became involved with drugs or alcohol to try to avoid the discomfort of depression. It didn't work for them and it won't work for you. Depression and alcoholism often run in families. The period following the suicide of a loved one can leave you vulnerable to alcohol and drug abuse. Be very aware of increased use and do not add them to your other problems.

Ignoring Your Health

When you are suffering the shock of loss you may neglect your own well-being. You will probably have disturbed sleep and loss of appetite. You might not get proper exercise. Your body will become run-down. Stress can manifest itself in a variety of physical symptoms including aches and pains.

You may believe that your physical problems are a punishment for "allowing" the suicide. You will be especially vulnerable to physical illnesses. Succumbing to illness is another form of self-destruction. You may avoid seeking medical attention.

Dorothy believed her severe intestinal pains were her punishment for not being a good enough wife to her husband who committed suicide. Focusing on the real pain helped her deal with the much more intense psychic pain of guilt and loss that she was experiencing. She could barely eat and she lost weight. No one thought too much about this because her symptoms were indicative of mourning. Feeling worthless, Dorothy didn't think of consulting a doctor. Eventually an ulcerative condition was diagnosed. Surgery, which might have been avoided if she had earlier medical attention, became necessary.

The Dangers of Self-Involvement

During mourning, you may find that you become extremely self-centered. Your own pain, grief, guilt, despair, and recovery from the suicide are the only things you want to think about or talk about.

It is difficult to be sensitive to the needs of others. Your relationships may become strained because mutual sharing disappears. Although most people in your life will be ready to tolerate the one-sidedness for a little while, this period will not last long. Your family and friends will feel as if they have lost you. They may ask you how long you are going to continue to be obsessively involved with your loss. They will say annoying things like, "It's been three months—shouldn't you be over it already?" What they really mean is, "When are you going to be yourself again? I miss the old you."

Many survivors are angry that their friends are unsympathetic to their intense pain and grief. They tell us that they feel neglected and that people say stupid and insensitive things to them. Even worse are those friends who don't speak of the loss at all. Even in your bereavement you need to be aware that others are looking to you for clues about what you need and want from them. No one wants to upset you further. Many fear that to speak of your loss will be a painful reminder. Friends may be fooling themselves into believing that there are times that you forget your pain. It is essential for you to give signals about how you wish to be treated.

Like many suicide survivors, Edna was still constantly thinking about her son two years after he took his own life. She was hurt and angry at her friends who no longer asked about how she was feeling every time they met. If she was not given an opportunity to speak of her son, she felt that her friends were being insensitive. She resented discussing a problem or concern that didn't focus on her son's death. Her friends had been very supportive in the first months after his death. She could not understand why they seemed less anxious to spend time with her now.

A support group helped her to see that her friends wanted her back. They missed the Edna who had always been interested in their concerns as well as her own. It might be hard, maybe even impossible, for her to be that way now, but she needed to at least acknowledge that her friends missed the old Edna.

Many survivors feel ostracized by others because of their loss. However, we urge you to recognize that if you feel deserted by your friends, one reason may be that through your grief you have inadvertently deserted them.

Chapter 8

When a Parent Commits Suicide

Hushed voices, rooms full of people, flowers, tears, pitying looks, hidden glances, embarrassed silences . . . and half forgotten in the corner—a child. The child cannot really take in what has happened but knows that something momentous is wrong. His mother cries, wrings her hands, and is embraced by many people, most of whom he has never seen before. Occasionally she remembers to hug him; sometimes it hurts when she does because she hugs so hard. Every time she looks at him she cries. His father is dead! No one can really make him understand what that means. He wishes his father would come in and help him understand. He wishes his father would come in so no one would be so sad anymore. He wishes that someone would remember to give him his lunch.

No one will tell him how his father died. Some say he was sick, but his father walked him to the school bus that very morning and he didn't look sick at all. Most look away when he asks, even his mother who usually answered all of his questions. Maybe he did something that made his father die. Maybe that's why no one will tell him the reason.

They give him some toys and tell him to go and play. No one else is playing. No one else seems to be sure what to do. He thinks he is sad. He knows he is frightened. He wonders if his mother will ever act like his mother again. He wonders if anything will ever be the same again.

Abandoned

M*other, father,* and *parent* are among the most emotionally charged words in our vocabulary. Parents stand between you and the world. They meet your needs, love you more unconditionally than anyone else ever will, and present you with your first and most lasting view of the world and yourself. They set standards and examples, both good and bad, for your behavior forever. When a parent dies, no matter how young or old you are at the time, you are left feeling that there is no one standing guard for you anymore. You are alone in a very profound way. Many people feel their own mortality only after the death of a parent.

Even when your real parents are not as perfect as you might wish, as long as they are alive there is hope that they will change and become the ideal parents that you long for. Someone is there looking after you. Someone cares about your triumphs and your defeats. Someone will cheer you on or, if needed, rescue you. The death of a parent destroys that hope forever. You feel abandoned by that person who, by giving you life, has implicitly promised to make it worth living.

When your parent seeks death through suicide, your sense

of having been abandoned increases immeasurably. That person upon whom you so depended appears to have deserted you by choice. You feel as if you have been told you were not worth staying alive for. Even in your grief and despair you feel resentment and rage at being left. No matter what your age or circumstance, no one can be prepared for this. How could this be done to you? How is it possible ever to come to terms with the idea that your parent did not feel that you were important enough to live for? "What does this suicide mean about me?" you ask yourself. "Was I so unloved or unlovable that I deserved to be left?" Feelings of abandonment by the suicide of a parent are difficult at any time in your life, but different life stages and circumstances present different problems for recovery.

Like Parent, Like Child?: Secrets Can Be Dangerous

Parents are our first and most important models of how to behave. For better or worse we seem to become more like our parents than anyone else. Who has not been surprised to find himself inadvertently imitating behaviors of his mother or father, even behavior that he disliked and rejected? You are less likely to notice the positive characteristics that your parents bequeathed you; you generally take credit for those traits yourself.

Families seem to produce certain recurring patterns. Tendencies for depression run in some families. It is well known that children who have been abused sexually or physically by a parent are more likely than others to become abusers of their own children even though they know the devastation of such abuse. Similarly, alcoholic parents frequently produce alcoholic children.

It has also been observed that suicidal behavior can run in families. For the purposes of this discussion it is not important to comment on whether environment or heredity is more or less responsible. It is important to know that when a child has had a parent commit suicide he is at an increased risk of choosing suicide as a solution.

It is well known that the death of a parent leaves one vulnerable to depression, and that the earlier the loss, the greater the vulnerability. When the death is from suicide the disruption in the family is even greater than with other types of death. It may be that the difficulty a family may experience in mourning a suicide leaves the children more vulnerable. It may be that once the taboo against suicide has been broken in a family it becomes more possible for other family members to act in the same way. Another explanation may be that a child wonders about her parent's life, tries to make sense of it, and thus thinks a great deal about a parent's suicide. She may in some way wish to connect or unite with her parent by imitating the act.

In the past, and to a lesser extent today, suicide has been a taboo subject. When a family member took his own life this fact was seldom admitted and rarely discussed. Nonetheless, everyone knew something was unsaid, but no one was permitted to break the silence. In this way the circumstances leading up to the suicide and people's feelings in the aftermath became even more intriguing, especially to children who always seem to know when there is something being kept from them. Family secrets not brought into the open tend to take on a life and power of their own as they fester in a child's mind. Long after everyone believes the secrets are forgotten, they can live in a child's mind.

When twenty-six-year-old Alan shot himself, just as his father had twenty-two years earlier, the family was in shock. Was it a bizarre coincidence or was Alan repeating his father's behavior? "But he couldn't have known," his mother cried. "We kept all that from him and his sister, Lee. He was only four and Lee was barely six. They couldn't possibly have understood."

But Lee said that she had guessed and that she and Alan had discussed their suspicions about their father's suicide many times while they were growing up. They believed that it must be something terribly shameful since no one ever spoke of it. They never talked about it with their mother, believing that since she never mentioned it she was unable to handle her own feelings. "How could she think we didn't know, since we were both in the house when it happened?" Lee pondered. "Mom never found a way to reconcile who my father had been with what happened to him."

Alan had been brought up believing lots of wonderful things about his father. He had been a thoughtful and sensitive man, someone to whom others turned in times of trouble. His mother taught him that his father had believed in life and living. He was remembered as a person who encouraged others to overcome difficulties and to not let anything stand in their way. Alan was encouraged to emulate these fine characteristics. In many ways he did.

After Alan's suicide, when the truth about her father's death came out, Lee told her mother that they were never able to understand how such a man could take his own life. Neither of them had ever heard the full story of their father's life. "Terrible accident" was how the death was described. The unspoken message was: "Don't ask anymore about this."

No one ever explained that Alan's father had had a history of depression and two hospitalizations after uncompleted suicide attempts—one when the children were barely more than infants. No one ever discussed that a failing business had been straining his marriage when he killed himself. No one mentioned that he had shown signs of slipping into depression again.

Just how Alan's father's suicide led to his son's similar death will never be clearly known. Was it genetically or biochemically predetermined? If so, we believe that if Alan knew more about what had happened to his father, if the family could have discussed the events or changes in his father that foreshadowed his suicide, Alan might have seen warning signs in himself and might have been able to do something about them. Alan did not know of his father's history of depressive episodes. He never had a warning that he might suffer from similar feelings.

Was it a case of imitative behavior? Alan had heard the message that you should try to overcome difficulties. His father's suicide demonstrated that if you cannot, taking your own life is a viable solution. It was the solution taken by someone he had been taught to admire. Why shouldn't he choose the same way out that his father did?

We often say that the tragedy of suicide is that it is a permanent solution to a temporary problem. Suicide cannot be thought of as a romantic or mysterious act. It must be viewed as the worst of choices made by a mind no longer able to function in a rational manner. It is imperative that the mystery, the drama, and the romance of the act be taken away through open discussion of both the life of the person who committed suicide and the feelings of those who are left behind.

There is strong precedent in our society not to speak ill of the dead. It is not speaking ill to help survivors understand as much as possible what led up to a suicide and to discuss other ways that apparently problems might be solved. You can talk about the anger that you feel toward someone who elects this way out without vilifying the person. If mental illness or depression were factors in leading to the suicide, then it is important to discuss getting help for these conditions. It is necessary to emphasize that seeking treatment is a wise, not a shameful, thing to do.

After Kay's mother took her own life, Kay, who was already an adult, attended a support group with her father. Neither attempted to romanticize what had happened. Her father openly discussed that Kay's mother had been seriously depressed for many years. She could never seem to find contentment or even relief from her depression no matter what she tried, and she had tried many things. Kay had loved her mother. Never had either parent tried to hide from her the fact that her mother was subject to incapacitating depressions.

Kay had lived with her mother's depressions for most of her life. She had been angry at her when she was growing up. She had felt deserted when her mother was in her depressed moods. Sometimes she believed that she was the cause of her mother's sadness. Kay tried to be a good little girl, but her mother got depressed anyway. Kay was lucky because her father had helped her understand that her mother's problems were not her fault.

Her father and mother had also taken her to family therapy sessions where she had been encouraged to talk about her feelings.

Kay also knew that her mother had a tremendous fear of being hospitalized, which was the treatment of choice for someone as depressed as she had become. By the time Kay was in high school, she understood that her mother would never willingly allow herself to go to a hospital. Both Kay and her father were angry that her mother had not been willing to be hospitalized. Along with their sorrow that Kay's mother had been in so much pain that suicide appeared to be her only way out, they were angry that she had abandoned them and the rest of their family. In this family suicide will be known as an unacceptable solution.

How members of a family cope with uncomfortable feelings or problem situations can be an important clue as to whether or not suicide will be chosen as a solution for serious crises. We have found that many of those who commit suicide have a history of burying or suppressing troublesome emotions rather than confronting them. They have tended to use alcohol or other substances among other means of escape. The excessive reliance on almost any form of activity may be a way of escaping from emotional conflicts or pain. If your parents' pattern was to avoid pain and conflict, it is important for you to think about whether this is your pattern also. Since you are reading this book, we can assume that you are thinking seriously about someone's suicide and are probably in some kind of pain. That you are using your thinking and reasoning ability to explore something about this kind of pain is a good sign. It suggests that you are not someone who immediately takes action to escape from pain but rather you are someone who can tolerate thinking about what is troubling you.

If you are the caretaker of a child whose parent has committed suicide, it is important to help that child be able to tolerate and face painful experiences without immediately taking actions to avoid that pain. No one lives a life without emotional conflict, crisis, anxiety, panic, or sadness. Talking to a child about the suicide of a parent encourages thinking, communicating, and sharing as ways of dealing with painful matters. To avoid these issues is to teach that pain is intolerable and should be avoided. Unfortunately, suicide is a surefire way never to have to feel pain again.

Talking to Children About Death and Suicide

In our society it is a common mistake to assume that we should not really talk to children about death because they are too young and cannot understand. Further, because they probably don't understand anyway, we should not burden them with such upsetting things. If many of us have trouble speaking of death, almost all of us find it impossible to speak about suicide.

Just because children do not speak about their feelings after a parent dies, does not mean that children are not deeply affected. Perhaps it is simpler to tell ourselves that we need not be concerned about a child's feelings, since we have trouble with our own feelings of loss. But childen who are not being verbal about what they are feeling may express themselves in other ways.

One of the most common changes you will notice in a child who has lost a parent is the need to cling excessively to the remaining parent or another significant person in the child's life. The child behaves as if she were fearful that this person might also disappear from her life. Separating to go to sleep at naptime or at night may become a frightening experience. The child who has not been helped to understand the death and to some extent how it came to happen will be especially afraid. For her, the temporary disappearance of a loved one could mean that person might never return.

The child needs to be told that his mother or father has died, which means that he or she will never come back again. He also needs to be told that the death had nothing to do with anything that he did. When the child asks, "How did my mommy die?" he needs to be told as simply, directly, and truthfully as possible. Even if he does not fully understand what you tell him at this time, you are laying the groundwork for fuller comprehension as he grows older and more able to understand what has been said to him.

One way to proceed is to tell him that mommy had a sickness that made her so sad that she did not wish to live anymore. It is essential to tell the child that, of course, everyone gets sad some of the time and that this is not the same as how sad his mommy was. She was so sad that she couldn't even think about anyone else and how much they would miss her. You can tell him that you are all sad that mommy is dead but that you know that it is important to keep on living. You can tell him that you are also sad that mommy did this and couldn't wait until she didn't feel so bad anymore, because you know that sadness is something that you can get over. Tell him that you know there are lots of ways to deal with bad problems and you are very sorry that mommy chose this way, which is not a good way. She chose a forever way, so she will never know that she could have found another way to deal with her terrible sadness. Make sure to tell him that if he is ever sad you will help him. Mommy was not a bad person, but you believe that she chose a bad way to solve her problems.

You must also make it clear that someone can get sick without dying. For most of the ways in which one gets sick there are many ways to get better. Sometimes you can get better all by yourself, but many times you will need someone to help you. There are many kinds of helpers, those that help with problems of the body and those that help with problems of the mind or feelings. Let the child know you will help him to find the right person if he ever has any of the kinds of sickness that will not get better by themselves.

Through your actions as well as your words you must let a

child know that she can speak about her mother, about the death, and about the way her mommy died any time she wishes to do so. Even though you are probably mourning the suicide as well, it is essential that you remain open to the child's distress. The worst thing that can happen to a bereaved child is that the adults deny the reality of what she is feeling.

A child should also be involved in the rituals surrounding his parent's death. He can learn that people can be very upset and that other people can comfort them. He will learn that something very important has happened, and when such important things happen, it is okay to take time out from your usual routine to find ways to deal with your feelings. The child who is sent right back to school or to a friend's house to play while the grown-ups mourn misses a crucial part of the experience of the death of a loved one. He misses the chance to share the experience of grief with others. He misses the chance to learn that people have a variety of feelings when a loved one dies and a variety of ways of expressing those feelings.

Many children wish to know in a very concrete way where mommy is now. The notion that she is in heaven with God can be comforting but is also quite abstract. A young child needs something more specific. A child can be taken to the cemetery and shown the place where his parent is buried. This also becomes the place he can go to communicate with his dead parent. This is the place he can bring the special picture that he made at school or leave flowers or other gifts.

If going to a cemetery plot is impossible, or if the parent has been cremated rather than buried, another kind of specific place where the parent's spirit resides can be created to fill this need. It will probably be a place that has had special meaning to either the parent or the child or both. For some it is a place that they liked to go together. For others it is a place that the parent was known to love, perhaps a place where he was known to go when he wanted to be alone with his own thoughts. The church or synagogue can be specified as the special spiritual place where one can communicate with a deceased parent.

Children's Actions
Speak Louder Than Words

Children are far less likely than adults to tell you how they feel. They probably won't even tell you directly that they are feeling badly, but they will show you. Any marked change in a child's behavior can be a signal of underlying discomfort. A distressed child often has trouble going to sleep at night or sleeping through the night. She will want to sleep with the surviving parent or a sibling. She may not be comfortable in her room as she once was. Frightening nightmares may waken her. Conversely, a child may withdraw from contact with others and may want to sleep more than usual. He may cling to old toys, stuffed animals, or pets to give him security and comfort. You should not try to interfere with this behavior but should see it as a clue that the child is fearful and unhappy.

How a child performs in the world outside of his home is an important clue to his feelings. The child who once did well in school but now seems to be having trouble is letting you know that something is not right for him. The child who is suddenly much more irritable and easier to anger than he previously had been is having a problem. The child who shuns friendships and spends increasing amounts of time alone and the child who loses interest in things that used to excite him is in trouble. An involvement with dangerous activities is another clue. Even if a child's parent committed suicide several years earlier, the suicide can still be causing trouble today. It is not unusual for a child's most pronounced reactions to occur quite a while after the suicide.

Helping While
You Feel Helpless

The tragedy for a child who loses a parent to suicide is that he loses both parents—one to suicide and the other to the aftermath of that suicide. When you have just lost a spouse to suicide it is difficult for you to be sensitive and comforting to your child. You will be lost in your own reactions for some time and will not have your usual ability to be tuned into your child's needs. Your child may feel abandoned by you at the time he needs you most. This is a time when the whole family needs all the outside support and help available. Aunts, uncles, cousins, and grandparents may be helpful supporters. However, they have also lost a family member to suicide and are struggling with their own reactions. Sometimes it takes someone outside of the family to help.

Psychotherapists, clergy, and bereavement support groups can be of assistance to your family. For younger children, especially the child who is not verbalizing many feelings, it is important to seek the services of a professional therapist who is skilled and trained to deal with young children. This therapist will know how to communicate with a child in her own language, which is play.

Tim, the youngest child in a large family, was five when his father committed suicide. His mother and older brothers and sisters were all pretty vocal about their feelings and their needs and were all pretty wrapped up in their own responses to the suicide. Tim might have been neglected except that he made himself known by becoming excessively clingy and fearful. He wouldn't let his mother out of his sight. He wouldn't sleep in his own bed at night. He wouldn't go to his grandfather's house. And he frequently and loudly insisted that he would definitely not be attending kindergarten ever again.

Tim's mother was seeing a therapist at the time. When the therapist heard the mother's complaints about Tim, she suspected the trouble was that no one was "listening" to the child's concerns about his father's suicide. She suggested that a trained child therapist spend some time with Tim.

Tim and his therapist didn't talk much at first, but they did play. His mother had said that Tim did not know anything about how his father had died, just that he was dead. Nonetheless, Tim began to play out with the therapist's dolls exactly how his father had commited suicide, letting her know that he knew all about it. They were able to talk about his concerns. She was able to give his mother some clues about what was on Tim's mind, and his mother was better able to be comforting and reassuring to her son. She was genuinely surprised that he knew and understood as much as he did. She and Tim spoke about the things they remembered and missed about dad, which was comforting and strengthening for each of them.

It's All My
Fault—Or Is It?

Children feel responsible for their parents much as parents feel responsible for their children. Our language is replete with expressions assigning blame for parental feelings and actions to children. Which of us has not said, in moments of extreme frustration, "Stop that! You're giving mommy a headache," or "If you do that it will kill your father"? The list of such statements is endless and even includes, "You'll be the death of me." These words will haunt children. Even when such statements have never actually been said, all children are well aware that what they do can have powerful effects on how their parents feel. Guilt for what has been done and for what has not been done becomes a painful legacy for the survivor.

Guilt is particularly intense if the parental suicide follows a bitter argument with a child. Even the surviving parent tends to place blame overtly or secretly at the feet of the offending child. Compassion and understanding, as well as an ability to accept that people can have difficult relationships, are necessary if families are to recover.

Robert, a man in his fifties, shot himself a few hours after having an intense fight with his sixteen-year-old son, Morris. His mother, who knew more about the whole picture than Morris did, lashed out at Morris also, implying that had they not fought so much, Robert would still be alive. Although she quickly denied that she really believed what she had screamed out in anger and shock, his mother's words stayed painfully with Morris. She avoided talking about her feelings with her son for a long time. She could not bring herself to think about or discuss some of the other reasons that she thought might have contributed to her husband's death. During that time Morris felt worse and worse. He felt that his mother had cast him out of the family and could not speak with him because he caused his father's suicide. In fact, his mother was so depressed over the suicide that she could pay attention to nothing but her own grief. She barely knew that Morris existed. Morris desperately needed someone but didn't know where to turn.

Morris had an Aunt Sarah, his mother's sister, with whom he was close. While she was supportive to Morris's mother, she was also very supportive to Morris. Aunt Sarah helped him to see that Robert had had strong needs to control everyone and everything around him. That trait had always been part of his personality. Morris was surprised to learn that his father's job had been in jeopardy. Morris also didn't know that his father was in poor health, making it unlikely that he would be able to find a comparable position elsewhere. His father's anxiety about his unsettled state increased his need to have control over whatever he could still control.

Robert had been born in another country and did not fully understand American ways, especially our attitudes toward teenagers and their relationship to parents and other authorities. He believed that a father must provide for his family and that a father's word was law. The more he felt that he was going to be unable to be the sole provider, the more he needed his word to be obeyed so that he would not lose all the roles of fatherhood. He was very upset that his wife had gone to work and was making as much money as he was. It was not surprising that Morris was having a stormy period as he struggled for autonomy.

As he learned more, Morris was able to believe that fighting with his father was barely relevant to his father's decision to commit suicide. He was able to reevaluate those fights and to see that it was important for him to struggle to loosen the unrealistic degree of control that his father expected to have over him. Finally, one of the hardest conclusions for Morris to reach was that even after he realized he absolutely could not have prevented his father's suicide, he also realized that he would have been unwilling to submit totally to his father's will. Coming to terms with that was important, for even though it could not have saved his father's life, it was essential for Morris to face the truth that he would not have surrendered his autonomy.

In examining your guilt you must ask yourself: Could I have made the choice to do what someone else needed me to do in order for them to refrain from taking their own life? Could I make that choice if it meant giving up something that was crucially important to me? And does anyone really have the right to put me in that position?

The child of a chronically depressed person feels a lifetime demand from that person to nurture and be a parent to the parent. This may require providing seemingly endless amounts of attention. Such a depressed person may be angry when attention is given to anyone else for whatever reason. Withdrawal of attention appears to increase the parent's depression and despair. Somewhere in the recesses of the child's mind may even lie the hidden fear that were he to withdraw attention his parent might indeed decide that there was nothing left to live for. What, he wonders, is his responsibility in this kind of a situation. Sometimes he may have even found himself wishing that his depressed, dependent, endlessly demanding parent would die—a thought he surely erased from his consciousness almost as quickly as it occurred and one that he would never want to admit to anyone. Nonetheless, it is a most human thought.

Lydia would have been a strikingly beautiful young woman had her eyes not been so red from continual crying. She had given birth to her first child two weeks earlier. The next day, her mother, Monica, locked herself in the garage in the car with the motor running and ended her own life. She had not been to see her only grandson whose birth she supposedly had been happily awaiting.

Monica had been chronically unhappy for many years. Doctor after doctor and many medications seemed to afford no relief from her continued depression. Lydia spoke with her almost every day and visited with her as often as she possibly could. She entertained, encouraged, and cajoled her mother. She had spent many years of her adult life at her mother's beck and call.

Lydia knew that when she had her own child she would not be able to be as available to her mother as she had been before. While she worried about this, she also knew that she and her husband wanted to have a child very much. She hoped that her mother would love her grandchild and that it might even give new hopefulness to her life.

When Monica chose to use her grandchild's birth as a signal to take her life, Lydia felt devastated with guilt. She feared that she had made a wrong choice and by doing so had caused her mother's suicide. She was frightened that she would always associate her baby's birth with her mother's death and might even come to resent her child.

No one can be expected to take complete responsibility for another's life. Lydia came to see that she had a right to live her own life. Far from abandoning her mother, she had attempted to include her mother in her life. What her mother seemed to need was far beyond Lydia's ability to give. Even had she continued to make her mother the focus of her life, there is no guarantee that Monica might not have made the same decision but on a different pretext.

After her guilt, Lydia had to deal with her anger at her mother's choice. She was angry that her child would never have her for a grandparent. She was angry that her child's birth, which should have been a joyous time for the family, was marred by the tragedy and grief of her mother's suicide. For Lydia, anger was a better emotion to be feeling than guilt.

Finally, Lydia had to feel grief about the loss of her mother, the same grief that anyone who loses a parent feels. She missed her. She missed the time that she spent with her. She missed being able to share the growth of her baby with her and she missed the advice her mother could have offered. She missed having a parent, even a troubled parent.

Picking Up the Pieces

The death of a parent is painful no matter when or how the death happens. You who are recovering from the suicide of a parent or helping a child to recover from the suicide of a parent face a twofold task: After you have dealt with the grief, guilt, anger, and blame of suicide, you are left to mourn the loss. Too often while you are dealing with the shock of suicide you forget to pay attention to your own profound sense of loss. Just when others are expecting you to be over it, you find yourself again realizing that your mother or father is dead and will not return.

Much healing takes place when you examine your parent's life and try to comprehend the pressures and pains that led him to his dreadful decision. Then you must understand the meaning of this loss in your own life. You will find that your thoughts turn from the dead parent to yourself. What will your life be like without your parent? What will replace the emptiness left by this death in your life? How will you go on without your parent? Once you are able to think about these things, you are beginning to recover and heal.

Chapter 9

When a Child

Commits Suicide

In the natural order of life, we expect to endure the death of our parents, hopefully after we have enjoyed them for many years. Following the same natural order, we expect to nurture our children and support them both physically and emotionally as they mature to adulthood. This natural order is painfully disrupted when a child dies. It may well be the most wrenching loss anyone can experience.

From the time of conception parents feel totally responsible for their children's well-being. This feeling never leaves, no matter how old the children are or how far away they live. If you lose a child to death everything in your life changes. You feel as if an important part of both your past and your future is gone. "How many children do you have?" becomes a painful, gut-wrenching question. Do you include your dead child in this number? Or do you say that you had a child who died, knowing that suicide will change a casual conversation into an intimate revelation that you are not sure you want to share. If you believe that you have any responsibility for that death your pain increases immeasurably.

I Must Be Guilty

If your child has taken her own life, guilt will be one of the most intense feelings. You will wonder what you did wrong. How did you fail your child? Inevitably you will review the past, over and over again, looking for the mistakes you think you have made to fuel your conviction that you are to blame for your child's suicide. Unfortunately, you will find things for which to blame yourself. No parent is perfect. No parent has been as attentive, as loving, and as supportive as he might like to have been.

We have listened to the self-recriminations of scores of bereaved parents: "I never should have gone to work. Perhaps if I had been at home more...." "Maybe if I had taught him to be more independent—I spent too much time with him. I wasn't like those mothers who go off to work and leave their children." "I was too hard a disciplinarian. I expected too much from my son." "I never expected anything from her. Whatever she wanted, so long as she was happy...." There are many different voices, one contradicting the other, each filled with pain and loss, each trying to find explanations for the inexplicable.

The reasons for your child's suicide are complex and, although many theories have been offered, no one really knows why some children and young adults choose to commit suicide whereas others do not. You are not likely to find definitive answers to your haunting questions.

In addition to looking for what you did wrong, you may also look for the signs you missed that your child was suicidal. With the clarity of hindsight you may even find some clues you did not recognize at the time. We believe that those people who have suicidal ideas and wish to be stopped will give out very clear messages of their intent. Others who are completely serious in their resolve that suicide is the only solution to their problem will fool everyone. Many suicide victims we have known of through their survivors had been examined by psychiatric professionals shortly before their deaths. Often they were brought for consultation by worried parents. Sometimes they were released from psychiatric hospitals because they were believed to be out of danger.

Can we assume that these professionals did not know what they were doing? We believe that a more realistic explanation is that these suicides were people intent on taking their own lives and that they knew enough to hide that fact from those who might have stopped them.

Andrea had been hospitalized for suicidal intentions. She attended a support group because she had lost a dear friend to suicide. She had met her friend in a psychiatric hospital. The group listened very intently the night that she explained how hospital patients learn what to say and what not to say if they wish to be discharged or let out on pass. "If you talk about wanting to kill yourself, or give hints to that effect, they'll keep you, but if you tell them that you have no such ideas they'll let you out. I'm sure that my friend, who always planned to take his own life one day, just told them he was over those ideas and then got out and did it."

Fear of Exposure

Fear of exposure is an aspect of guilt. You feel as though your child's suicide exposes you to the world as an unfit or unworthy parent. You may be convinced that others are making that judgment of you. Society often blames parents for their children's failures and problems. This attitude is changing as scientists learn more about why people behave as they do. As we have said previously, no theory exists that adequately explains why some people commit suicide.

After years of working with families who survive the suicide of a son or daughter, no clear patterns about parents or how they failed have emerged. In fact, these parents appear to be struggling with family problems that, up to the point of suicide, are not appreciably different from those of parents we meet who come to therapy for a variety of other reasons.

Blame: If It's Not My Fault, It Must Be Yours

Our culture leads us to believe that for every effect a cause can be determined. When the effect is a bad one, like the suicide of a child, cause becomes blame. The first person you are likely to blame is yourself. After you have examined your guilt you will look for someone else to blame. That person is usually the child's other parent: your husband or wife. Just as you can recall the "mistakes" you made while raising your child, you can be as clear, perhaps clearer, about what your spouse did wrong. At a time when you need to share your grief with each other you may become bitter antagonists engaged in mutual blame. It is not surprising that many marriages do not survive the suicide of a child.

You may find that you are afraid to let anyone know how angry you are at your spouse, especially him. You may not wish to cause him more pain than he is already feeling. You may be afraid that sharing your feelings will make him angry. You may believe that you need to protect him from the truth as you see it. You may even be afraid that if you tell him what you believe he did wrong, he will feel free to point out the mistakes that you are tormenting yourself for making. There is also the fear that if all these feelings were known your marriage might not survive. You have just suffered a devastating loss and are not sure you can stand another.

When you avoid discussing your feelings with someone as important to you as your husband or wife, chances are that you will find yourself becoming isolated. Your behavior will become forced and insincere. Your anger, rather than being hidden, will probably gain expression in indirect, hostile ways. You may believe that by keeping your troubling thoughts to yourself you will help maintain your relationship, but the opposite is true. Covering up or avoiding these difficult feelings leads to loneliness.

We recommend that if you are angry at your spouse because you blame him for the suicide of your child, you must find a way to speak with him about these feelings. Only by expressing your angry recriminations can you arrive at reconciliation and forgiveness. You may be surprised to find that what you blame him for is far less serious than what he believes he has done. Nothing can bring back your child and nothing can undo what has been done in the past. However, only when each of you can acknowledge that you both feel some guilt and some blame can you forgive yourself and each other and rebuild your life together.

Often the couples who are most openly angry with each other after the suicide of their child come to the most workable reconciliations. Bill and Linda were each brilliant and successful in the same profession. After their eighteen-year-old daughter took her own life they used some of their brilliance to dissect the mistakes the other had made while raising her. It was clear that they had once loved each other very much. Each one was in great pain over the loss. At first they could not bear to voice their anger. They still cared enough about each other to shrink back from the pain that their words would cause. Because they held back they were unable to comfort each other or share memories of their daughter's life or help each other to make any sense of what had happened. Although they treated each other cordially, it was clear to everyone that the politeness barely masked the hostility and rage that each felt but both denied.

After a few therapy sessions, the hidden feelings burst forth from Linda, followed quickly by retaliations from Bill. They screamed at each other until they were exhausted. They were surprised that the words they said to each other were no different from the quarrels they had always had about how to raise their daughter. The only thing that changed for them once they had heard each other's accusations was that they no longer needed to be afraid of what the other was thinking. Now they could find ways of forgiving and supporting each other. They were still angry at each other some of the time, but now they could talk about it. The worst had been said and they decided they could still live with each other. Before they had fought openly, neither had been sure that their marriage could survive their anger, a loss neither had been willing to risk.

Relief

Guilt is a reaction you expect after a suicide. A sense of relief is not. This feeling may come as an unwelcome surprise, a shock. Many survivors are ashamed to admit feeling relieved to anyone and they keep this emotion a secret.

However, it is not really so surprising that survivors feel relief. Suicide does not occur in a vacuum. Suicide does not happen at a time when everyone is happy. Suicide is usually the culmination of a sequence of troubled and troubling events, which can be very disruptive to a family, especially when a child is involved. The precursors of suicide often include alcohol or drug abuse, school difficulties, parent–child problems, agitated depressions, problems at work, conflicts with friends, or problems with the law. Parents have often been embroiled in bitter battles or have felt helpless, unable to make a difficult situation better. Frequently, outside helpers have been engaged to solve the problems, requiring a considerable financial and emotional investment. Often the troubles have persisted for a long time. The suicide ends that period of turmoil and constant worry. Mothers and fathers have shamefully told us that at least they no longer worried what the next phone call would bring, for the worst had already happened.

Marvin is a thoughtful man who takes his responsibilities to his family seriously. He also feels a commitment to his neighbors and his community. His son became heavily addicted to drugs during his college years. In addition to the concerns he had for his son's well-being, he worried constantly about the damage his son might do to others as a consequence of being addicted. Each time his telephone rang, two thoughts competed in Marvin's mind: Would this call be news of something terrible having happened to his son, for example, a drug ovedose, or would it be news of his son injuring someone else, for example, in an automobile accident?

Marvin and his wife took all the steps they could think of to help their son. They did not want him to die or to be destroyed by his addiction. Marvin admitted that one of the feelings he had when his son died was relief that he had not harmed anyone.

If you are a surviving parent who sometimes feels this way, you probably believe that you are an abnormal mother or father and you do not want anyone else to know. You may suspect that you are the only parent who has ever had these feelings. That is not the case. It is natural to feel relieved when a difficult problem is solved, even when the solution brings more problems and grief in its wake.

Anger

Feeling angry after the suicide of a child is common to survivors, who often feel ashamed of having these feelings. You may be angry at your child for leaving you. The instant separation from someone you loved and nurtured may leave you feeling helplessly enraged with no target for your anger. You may wish that you had been party to the decision being made. You may believe that you could have talked her out of it, helped her to find a better solution.

You may also be angry about the way in which your life has been changed. Your hopes and dreams for the future of your family have been shattered. The fantasies you may have enjoyed about the pleasures your child could bring have turned into nightmares. Rage is a natural response to the bitter harvest of pain and devastation that is the result of all the effort you put into raising a child. Parents who have made their children the entire focus of their lives and have based their own self-esteem on what their children achieve will be the most angry and have the most difficulty rebuilding their lives.

Matt and Eve seemed like the kind of parents that every child should have. Others admired and envied their devotion to their two daughters, feeling guilty when then could not give as much of themselves to their children as these two did. Eve baked cookies, was a Brownie and Girl Scout leader, organized the car pools, and sewed beautiful costumes whenever they were needed. Matt coached the soccer and softball teams and took his daughters to theaters and museums. Evenings were spent helping the girls, especially Andrea, with her homework. They knew that Andrea was a slow learner who was insecure and they did everything they could to help her feel better about herself. When things went well for the children, Matt and Eve felt gratified. There was not much else in their lives that seemed to matter.

When Andrea was eighteen she took her own life. Her parents were inconsolable. Their other daughter could not be around them without feeling their pain, so she stayed away from home as much as possible and soon afterward moved into an apartment of her own. Matt and Eve felt that Andrea had taken not only her life but theirs along with it. They felt very angry and cheated. After all, they had devoted their whole lives to these children. For several years they bemoaned their fate and spoke only of what devoted parents they had been. It was as if their lives had stopped and they could find no way to get going again. Gradually they came to see that it was up to them to find new ways of giving meaning to the rest of their lives. Though it was far from easy, they were eventually able to do so. Perhaps for the first time they asked themselves what they liked to do and how they liked to spend time. The answers surprised them. Matt took up photography and began a second career photographing events for other families. His sensitive photographs were sought after in his community. Eve became a volunteer on a crisis hot line. She got great satisfaction from helping others who were having problems.

Anger can be a healthy response to your child's suicide. It means that you can still think of yourself and the life that is still yours to live. Your child's suicide does not mean that your life has to come to an end also. One couple remembers that one of the first things they said to each other after learning of their son's death was, "We will survive. We will not let this ruin what is left of our lives. We will not let this spoil our pleasure with our other children." It was not always easy for them to keep this promise to each other. At times it seemed impossible. But they saw the promise as a goal that they constantly worked toward achieving.

Gloria, in her mid-fifties, came to believe that her daughter Alice had found the peace through suicide that she had never found while she was alive. She even felt some relief that her troubled daughter was no longer in pain. There were no more tormented phone calls, no more emergency trips to wherever Alice was living to try to bring her comfort and support. What Gloria could not get over was her rage that Alice had deprived her mother of sharing the rest of her life with her daughter. Now there would never be any grandchildren. Now Gloria would never have the pleasure of watching her daughter come to terms with her demons and develop the potential that had been there when she was a laughing little girl.

Gloria felt guilty about these selfish concerns and could not share them with anyone, especially her husband. Her recovery was impeded by the feeling that she must be an unnatural mother for feeling this way. When Gloria finally dared to speak about these feelings at a support group meeting, she was surprised to find that several other mothers and fathers at the meeting felt the same way. Her husband also became more open about his anger at what their daughter had done; he felt that she had deprived him of having pleasures too. Gloria learned that he became teary-eyed whenever he saw pictures of the father of the bride dancing with his daughter at a wedding. He had long dreamed of sharing a similar moment with his daughter and now it would never come.

Sharing their feelings did nothing to change the pain they felt or to recover what they missed, but it relieved them of the burden of keeping some of their feelings hidden. Sharing brought this couple closer together in their grief. Instead of avoiding discussions, they now engaged more fully in mourning their losses. They were able to share fantasies about what Alice's life would have been like.

You Are Still a Parent

After the suicide of one of your children it is often hard to be a parent to your surviving children. Overcome with grief and depression you may have periods when you find it difficult to attend to the most minimal details of living. You may feel like you want to hide yourself away and not face anyone ever again. Getting out of bed in the morning may feel like a major accomplishment, and making a meal or going to the office can seem like something you will never be able to do again.

These feelings are normal and will eventually pass, but until they do you must give some thought to what is happening to your other children. To help you understand what your children may be experiencing we suggest you read chapter 11. You will see that your children are not only suffering the loss of a brother or sister but are suffering the loss of parental attention at a time when they need it most.

Family members will mourn their loss in their own ways. You may wish to speak constantly of the child that you have lost as a way of keeping him alive. Survivors have said that they are afraid if they forget about their lost child for one minute, he will slip into an abyss and be forgotten. It is completely understandable that you may not be ready to let go. Your children may feel differently. It may be hard for them to discuss their dead sibling and it may be equally hard for them to see their parents so upset.

Your children may believe that if they don't speak of their dead sibling, you will forget your pain and feel better. They may even resent that you think more about the child you have lost than you do about those who are living. Yes, you are still a parent, even though your pain may not be allowing you to fulfill those responsibilities. You may even want to believe that your other children are better off without you because you are so unsure of your ability to be a good parent to them. The knowledge that you are still needed as a parent can be the motivation for recovery that you need to shake you from despair.

Until you are ready to resume being even a minimal parent, it is important that someone serve as a substitute for a while. The problem is that the people most likely to do this, such as grandparents, aunts, uncles, or close family friends, are also suffering from the loss of your child. However, some of these people may be able to be helpful in supporting your children if they are asked to do so. You must recognize that it is completely understandable for you to admit that you are unable to be fully functional at this time. You need some time to begin to heal. You can even be open and direct with your children about this fact. Explain that you have asked Grandpa or Aunt Sally to come and stay for a while because you don't feel able to take care of them right now, and until you do, you want to make sure that their needs are being met. It is all right for the children to know that you are very upset; it will give them permission to feel as badly as they need to feel. You cannot pretend that your child's suicide has not had a profound impact on the family.

As we have said, the suicide of your child may shake your confidence in your ability to be a good parent to your other children. If you believe that you must have done something horribly wrong for this to have happened, you will begin to question your ability to do anything right as a parent. You may tend to give up providing guidance and assistance to your children because you believe that you have been a failure. But your children still need you to be their mother or father; you must fight the tendency to abandon responsibility. This is a good time to get support from others about your decisions while you rebuild your confidence.

Survivors have found that they are overly protective of their other children, fearing that they too may become suicidal. They may put pressure on their other children to be perfect, so they may be reassured of their parenting ability. They may also want the world to see them as unflawed, in order to combat public opinion that they must have been bad parents to have raised a child who would commit suicide. This pressure is unfair. Children will be resentful and rebel.

It is only natural for your child's suicide to become the central theme of your life. It colors everything that happens for a long time after the event. Some families find that life centers on keeping the memory of what happened alive. This may work for you, as parents, but it is not likely to be acceptable to your other children. They want to return to normalcy as soon as they possibly can. They will not want their identity always to be the brother or sister of the suicide.

Tess and Hal lost their older son, Brian, to suicide. Ken, their younger son, was eleven at the time. Tess was very angry at Hal, blaming him for their son's death. She believed he had been too harsh in his discipline of Brian and that he did not understand Brian's problems. Hal believed Tess had been too lax, too prone to excuse Brian's shortcomings. He believed she had ignored signs that Brian was using illegal drugs and had defended him too readily. Neither had much confidence left in their ability to raise a child. As a result of these feelings, as well as their depression, they didn't pay much attention to Ken.

Ken was a serious child, with his own desire to do well in school and in sports. For a time he was able to keep going pretty much on his own. He wanted his parents to be happy again. He didn't want to make more trouble for them than they already had. He didn't let them know how much he missed doing things as a family as they had before Brian's suicide.

When Ken began high school, things changed for him. He was faced with a new set of pressures and had important decisions to make about how he was going to live his life. He needed the guidance and support of his parents, which they were not giving him. They did give him all the money and all the freedom he wanted, believing these things would make up for their being unable to be parents to him.

Hal feared that his second son might get into some of the same difficulties as Brian but felt unable to help him. After all, nothing that he had done had helped Brian. He wasn't going to make those mistakes again. Tess, who was just starting to emerge from two years of deep depression, started to be aware that she had another son. She seemed resentful that Ken might need some attention from her. She felt as if she had already suffered enough.

It was not until the principal called to say that Ken had come to school drunk one morning that his parents were shocked into realizing that they were still needed as parents. The high school principal knew the family history. She suggested that professional therapy could help them sort things out. Luckily, Tess and Hal agreed and found someone who could help them.

Ken was able to let his parents know that he needed them. He didn't blame them for his brother's suicide, even if they blamed themselves and each other. He believed that they had tried to help Brian, but for some reason Brian was not able to be helped. Ken was afraid that they were not helping him because they believed that he, too, was doomed and he didn't want to be.

It was not easy for Tess, Hal, and Ken to become a working family group again. They had to face many difficult feelings about themselves and each other. They had to come to terms with Brian's suicide and the part each believed he had played in it. They had to forgive themselves and each other for what came before and after Brian's death. In time they were able to do so. Brian was lost to them, but Ken was not.

Chapter 10

When a Spouse Commits Suicide

There are no goodbyes, no chances for reconciliation or under-standing, not even the bitter recriminiations of divorce court. Your spouse is gone and you are left with guilt and self-doubt. Who was this person you married? What didn't you see or know about? What didn't you do to prevent this tragic ending to your most important relationship?

Why Did He Leave Me?

Not surprisingly, most husbands and wives feel abandoned when a spouse commits suicide. To have been part of a couple, for better or worse, and to now be alone, is to feel utterly rejected. What could have been so wrong with him or with you that he felt it necessary to take his own life? This question will trouble you for a long time to come. You may never find an answer, because the reasons that lead to suicide often remain unknown.

Although the question, "Why did he leave me?" is probably the one foremost in your mind, the question, "Why did he leave himself?" is the one you should be asking. We believe that when someone commits suicide he is no longer thinking of anyone except himself. He has ceased to believe that you or anyone else is part of his life. For him, at that moment, you no longer exist. If he were able to think of you, to connect with you, to empathize even for an instant with the pain he will cause you by his action, he could not possibly do what he did. If he could even remember that someone will care about what he is about to do he could not take that final step. All he can think about in those final seconds is erasing the terrible distress that he is feeling.

People who are very serious suicidal risks or those who have been prevented from successfully completing a suicidal act at the last moment frequently describe feeling as if they were in a dark tunnel. This tunnel is the visible manifestation of the prison of their own despair. They believed that they had an unsolvable dilemma. Their own act of self-destruction was the light at the end of the tunnel.

Should I Follow Her Lead?

You, who are the survivor of someone who felt strongly enough to take her own life, may find that kind of thinking almost impossible to understand. Every part of you is crying out that this logic is not true. What could possibly be so awful that a solution could not be found? Again and again the phrase "permanent solution to a temporary problem" goes through your mind. "We could have found a better answer" is what you continue to believe.

You are having healthy thoughts. Yours are the thoughts of a rational mind. Yours are the thoughts of someone who can still feel some positive connections to someone else and some hope for the future, even at the time of your deepest despair.

Your spouse, for whatever reason, was no longer able to feel this way. She saw no future. She could no longer see beyond a painful present. Even if she had been someone who had been able to overcome adversity and struggle against misfortune or troubles, she no longer felt capable of doing so. She saw suicide as the only possible solution to her problem. If, as you read this, you are still screaming inside that you cannot possibly understand how someone could feel this way, you are very lucky, because it is not a good way to feel. It is not a rational feeling. For any problem, an alternative solution can be found. Should there come a time when you also feel this desperate, you should be very frightened and should seek professional help immediately.

I Don't Deserve to Go On Living

When your spouse takes his or her own life it is probable that you will blame yourself. One of the most troublesome feelings you will have is that you were not worth staying alive for. You may believe that you were so unacceptable that to separate from you he needed to be dead. You may sometimes feel that you no longer have any right to be alive or to take part in the normal activities of living. This feeling is known as survivor's guilt. It comes over you the moment you notice you are feeling other things besides pain. You may feel it is inappropriate for you to even take pleasure in a sunset or to laugh at a funny movie.

Diane was bereft when her young husband shot himself shortly after they had argued. She blamed herself for saying hurtful things during the fight, things she really didn't mean. "How could he have taken me seriously?" she wondered. "I always said stupid, dramatic things when we fought, and I always took them back an hour later. Why couldn't he wait that hour this time?"

She believed that her life, too, ended with his gunshot. She thought about taking her own life. She felt that if she were not lovable enough to stay alive for, then maybe she didn't deserve to remain alive. She spoke so much about wanting to be dead that her parents took her to see a therapist immediately. But no matter how distressed she felt about her husband's death, no matter how guilty and self-blaming she became, she could not imagine being dead. To her, the actual decision to commit suicide remained unfathomable. Although for quite some time she saw no reason for living, her instinct for self-preservation kept her going.

Diane remained very depressed for a long while. She attended a support group for suicide survivors because her parents dragged her there. It was one of the few times during the week that she left her home. The other time was when she saw her therapist. At the support group she met others who understood her pain and self-recriminations. They understood that even though she was a stunningly beautiful young woman, she believed that her life would never return to normal and that she would forever hide in her parents' home as she did at the start of her bereavement.

Gradually Diane came to see that she would never be able to comprehend what had motivated her husband to pull the trigger that ended his life and irrevocably changed hers. The closest she came to an understanding was when she realized that his act of self-destruction had to do with something inside of him and not with anything that she had made him do. She may have said some very harsh things to him, but her words did not kill him; his pulling the trigger ended his life.

Now she could begin to re-create her life. She stopped being afraid that she would kill herself. She was still very sad about her terrible loss, but she believed she had a right to continue with her life.

But How Could
He Do This to Me?

You may be surprised to find that one of your strongest feelings is anger toward your dead spouse. Rather than feeling sorry that he felt unhappy enough to end his life, you are enraged at being abandoned. It is normal to be wondering what his suicide means to you. You feel angry that he apparently had so little regard for you that he could leave you alone. You are left to face your children, family, and friends as a widow. You feel as if you have been told you are not worth living for. You wonder if you will dare to be close to anyone again. You may be thinking that others see you as such a despicable person that your spouse believed it was better to die than to continue to live with you. You may even be making that judgment yourself. You may be feeling unworthy. Whatever self-doubts and insecurities you may have had before are greatly magnified now.

Anger is a normal response to being abandoned. It is the other face of guilt and self-reproach. Some degree of anger is necessary to motivate your recovery. If you remain mired in depression, which many believe is caused by anger directed inwardly, you will not feel that you deserve to continue with your life. You may even believe that you are unworthy of accepting the support and comfort of others. Feeling angry permits you to take the actions you need to take in order to go on. Anger is when you feel, "How dare he do that to me?" rather than, "I am so awful that I deserve to be miserable." Even being able to ask the question, "How could he do this to me?" suggests that you do not believe you deserved to have this happen to you. If you did, you would not be asking this question.

Paul was shattered by his wife Carleen's suicide. He was well aware that she suffered from recurring depressive episodes. He had supported her through many bouts with black moods, nonfunctional days, and sleepless nights. Expenditures for doctors and medications for depression were a regular part of their budget. When she was not in the midst of a depression, they shared a good life together.

At first, after Carleen died, Paul became quite depressed himself. He blamed himself for not being able to do even more for her. He magnified his shortcomings into major sins. In thirty years of marriage he had disappointed her many times. Each time seemed to come back with painful clarity now.

The day she took her life he had been at a business meeting, which seemed important at the time, and he had refused to leave it to come home earlier, as she had asked him to do. He had left meetings and canceled appointments many times for her—so many times, in fact, that his job was on the line. This time he believed that Carleen could wait a few more hours for him to come home. She said nothing directly about suicide, and he was fearful of risking his job. Later, Paul recalled that her last words to him during that telephone call had been, "Remember that I love you," which was an unusual way for her to end a conversation. "She must have been saying goodbye, and I didn't realize it." He was tortured by the thought that he could have saved her life if only he had made a different decision. He blamed himself for her death and refused to take comfort from anything that was said to him. Paul thought of himself as selfish and heartless and, in the depths of his own despair, he even felt as if he were as responsible as if he had murdered her.

Feeling that way, Paul could do nothing but mope around his home. He went unshaved and unwashed. He neglected his children, who needed to feel close to their father at this time even though they were all grown and living on their own. They would have liked his help in understanding their mother's death. They also would have liked some reassurance that he was going to survive this tragedy. He could give them nothing. He needed support from them but was feeling too much self-loathing to ask for it.

When I first came to meet him, he wore disheveled clothing. For the first months that he attended support group meetings he looked the same way. His clothing, his demeanor, and his words all said that he had lost respect for himself. He believed that he had failed to keep his wife alive. He believed that her suicide proved that he was not someone worth living for.

One evening a man came to the group impeccably groomed and dressed. I didn't recognize him, but he apparently knew me and the other group members. It was Paul. That night he told us, "I was always the best husband that I could be. I didn't deserve to be left the way I was. She never even said she was feeling like killing herself. She didn't give me a chance. If I had known that, of course I would have done whatever I could to stop her. For that I am angry. I am angry that her death took my life away. She made that choice. I didn't".

He continued, "I've been going around feeling like I deserve to be cursed and damned. I wouldn't even clean myself up because I was such an unworthy person. When I came out to the group I would deliberately look as bad as I could so that everyone could see the low esteem in which I held myself, the same low esteem in which I thought everyone must hold me.

"Well, I know now that I don't deserve that at all. I cared a lot about Carleen and proved it to her in many ways. I did my best for her and sometimes that was pretty good. What she did, she did. I didn't take her life and I am no longer going to let her take mine. I miss her. I'll always be sad that she is gone. I'll probably think of her every day for the rest of my life, but I am going to have a life."

Paul had been blaming himself. He noticed that he didn't blame anyone else in the group for the suicides of their loved ones. He always advised them not to feel so guilty, that the suicides of their loved ones were not their fault. If it were true for them, perhaps it could also be true for him. If you will permit youself to see what you have done for your spouse, you will begin to heal.

Paul realized that he was lonely. He began to look around for other women to have relationships with. Should he tell them how he had lost his wife? He worried that when he did, he might be seen as some sort of vile man women would run away from. It didn't happen that way. Paul was seen as warm and compassionate. He was soon seeing several women, although he was not ready to become seriously involved yet.

Once he had regained some sense of self-esteem, he was able to spend more time with his four children. He found out that they did not blame him for their mother's suicide as he feared they would. Together they could recall Carleen's life, remembering the good times as well as the difficult ones. As they understood her history they each could begin to make some sense of her choice to take her own life. No one in the family believed that it was a good or even sensible choice, but they came to see that it was hers.

Everyone Thinks It's My Fault

To the rational, normal, functioning mind, suicide is such an irrational, incomprehensible, senseless act that it is hard to believe anyone, especially someone you knew and loved, could make that choice. Almost all survivors blame themselves. You know how painful and self-destructive this can be.

One way to escape from this pain is to assign the blame to someone else. Many people will, unfortunately, blame the husband or the wife. It is simple and self-serving for others to believe that if you had been a better husband or wife the suicide would never have happened. As we have previously discussed, you may even feel this way yourself. First, you must stop believing the suicide is your fault. Then you will be better able to be sympathetic with those who take this attitude, without agreeing that it is the case.

Many husbands and wives have even been investigated as possible murderers of their dead spouse. In some places it appears to be standard police procedure to suspect the spouse until there is an official ruling of suicide. Unfortunately, this process accentuates your guilt. Remembering that this is a standard procedure after a sudden death may help you to stop believing that others actually think you were responsible.

The people most likely to hold you responsible are your spouse's parents. Besides you and your children, they are probably the people who are suffering most. If you are ready to empathize with their pain you can read chapter 9. Like you, parents will blame themselves. They will be wondering where they went wrong in raising a child who could take this action. The easiest way for them to excuse themselves is by feeling that he or she did not commit suicide when living as a child in their house, so it must be that you were not a good enough wife or husband. You are the handiest person around to blame. They may have said cruel and hurtful things to you. They may say they don't want to have anything to do with you. You may want to be distant from them also.

If your spouse's parents feel that way it will be hard to maintain a good or even workable relationship with them at this time. You may even add to the difficulty by believing they were the cause of the suicide. You may feel that if they had been better parents this would not have happened.

Many families find that after a suicide, instead of coming together for mutual support, surviving spouses and their in-laws are angry and blame each other. In some families this is said quite overtly; in others these same feelings remain as hidden undertones. Sometimes the families break apart permanently. Particularly when there are no children or grandchildren, families seem to find it hard to be comforting and caring rather than blaming and distant.

When there are children, it is especially important for the surviving parent and grandparents to maintain a sense of family. For the child, your spouse's parents remain an important link to past history. Your children have been left the legacy of suicide.

They will struggle to understand how their parent could do this. Knowing grandparents is an important way in which children can understand their parent's life.

Grandparents can be supportive in many ways. When you lose a spouse you lose someone who shares the financial and emotional responsibilities of raising children and even of caring for yourself. It is important that you and your spouse's parents be able to speak with each other about feelings. It is not an easy thing to do when everyone is in so much pain about the suicide. You must all be ready to give up the notion that someone is to blame. Everyone falls short of perfection.

There is a story about a couple who were asked on their fiftieth anniversary if they had ever considered divorce. "Murder yes, divorce no," was the reply.

Anyone who commits suicide was a troubled person at least some of the time. Such people are not easy to live with. Those of you whose spouses suffered from a series of depressions suffered right along with them. It is not easy to live with someone who is depressed. Certainly you were angry because of this burden. Surely you wondered how long you would be stuck in this situation.

In the aftermath of a suicide these feelings and statements come back to haunt you. Try to remember that many married people can recall screaming, "Go kill youself" or something like that to their mates. You are no different. Everyone in a relationship has wishes to be free at some time. This does not mean you caused the suicide.

We Weren't Married

Our society has few guidelines for responding to mourners who are not married. They may be engaged, separated, or divorced, may live together, or may even be lovers of whom the official family is unaware. If you are part of this group, you know the heartache of being an unacknowledged mourner. Sometimes it may seem as if there is just so much comfort to go around and the official family members want all there is for themselves. You are also likely to be the recipient of much of the blame for the suicide. It is not unusual for the family to close ranks and to exclude you as you become a convenient scapegoat. It is their way of dealing with their own pain and sorrow. You must be careful not to accept that distorted version of the suicide.

Remember that even official spouses often derive little comfort from the family of the suicide victim. It is imperative that you find support and comfort from your own resources. You have as much right to consider yourself as bereaved as anyone else, even if you are not given a place in official ceremonies. Do not let anyone imply that your feelings are less valid than theirs.

Andrew had shared his life with Jane for nine years before she committed suicide. Four years earlier, he had nurtured her through a six-month bout with an incapacitating depression, and he was trying to do so again when he came to her apartment and found that she had shot herself. Andrew had been asking Jane to live with him for many years. He had wanted them to be married but Jane refused because of her unstable emotional condition. She didn't want to be a burden to Andrew.

Andrew was grief-stricken. He blamed himself for not having taken better care of her, even though he had done everything he could possibly do. He wanted to be close to Jane's family and to mourn with them. They had all lost someone whom they loved very much. He had always been considered a member of the family before this happened.

At Jane's funeral, arranged entirely by her parents, he felt excluded and ostracized. Her parents acted as if he had no business being at the service and he was not allowed to sit with the family or to act as an official mourner. When he tried to spend time with the grieving family after the funeral, he was treated like an intruder. Jane's father had her apartment sealed and did not allow Andrew access, even though many of his personal belongings were there. He did not allow Andrew to take anything as a memento of Jane.

Her family's attitude toward him changed completely from what it had been before. They now acted as if he were the cause of her suicide. Several times he overheard remarks, such as, "This never would have happened if she had been married." Her mother acted as if she believed that Andrew would be happy now that Jane was gone and he could find someone new. Jane's sister and brother also were angry at Andrew and shunned him.

At first Andrew could not believe what was happening. He had not only lost Jane but a family he had come to love as his own. He was an only child whose parents had both died several years before. After disbelief, his response was retaliatory rage. As much as they blamed him for Jane's death, he found reasons to hold them responsible.

His rage interfered with his grieving. As long as his emotions could focus on being angry and blaming toward Jane's parents, he could avoid mourning the loss of the woman he loved. Anger at her parents, in some ways, kept Jane alive.

Andrew was lucky enough to come to a support group where others who had had similar experiences could help him to see what was happening. In the group were a couple who had started out blaming their son's girlfriend for his suicide in the same way that Jane's parents blamed Andrew. As Andrew came to understand the Browns, he was able to understand what was going on in his own life. He was strong enough to go to Jane's parents and tell them what he believed was happening. He said he loved them and believed they needed each other to survive this difficult time. To his surprise they were able to hear and accept what he was saying. Once they all stopped blaming one another, they could all cry and remember Jane together. They were able to come to a fuller understanding of her life and struggles. Although none of them can understand what made Jane decide to take her life, they have been able to agree that no one was at fault. They may have lost Jane, but they still have each other. Unfortunately, the ending to Andrew's story is not typical, but it does offer hope that reconciliations can happen.

Going On

One day you will come to accept that your spouse is dead and you are not. You can make the choice to go on with your life. You may even find there are things you can do now that were not possible while your spouse was alive. That you can now do these things may feel wrong to you, but allowing yourself to do them is part of your recovery.

Your spouse's family may be the ones most troubled by your attempts to begin a new life. Although they may be able to accept you and to be supportive if you are a grieving widow, they will probably have more trouble when you become involved in the living world, especially if you begin to date again. Many widows and widowers look for relationships with the opposite sex to ease their loneliness. You know that your involvement with new friends does not negate, in any way, the relationship you once shared with your spouse. His or her family usually sees these new relationships as meaning that you are already forgetting their loved one. They may believe you can callously replace him and go on with someone else. You can be sensitive to this fear and reassure them, before they ask, that this is not so. His family also needs to know that you will still be attached to them.

Children can be as threatened as parents when you begin to socialize again. It will seem to you as if they want you to remain a grieving widow forever. They have only known you as part of a married couple they knew as parents. They are afraid to find out that you can be anything else. Your children need the reassurance that you will always be a parent to them even if other things in your life change. It will take them time to accept these changes, but they will do so eventually.

Chapter 11

When a Sibling Commits Suicide

Few share the warp and woof of our lives like brothers and sisters. You share bedrooms and chores, family celebrations and family tensions, a history and a heritage. Bound by love and jealousy, you stick up for and fight with one another. You grow up together, sharing everything. You are always connected unless death do you part.

The death of a brother or sister not only destroys the fabric of a family as it has been, but it emphasizes one's own mortality. Older generations are supposed to die, not your own. When a sibling takes his or her own life the effect on the entire family is shattering.

This trauma challenges family beliefs and values as well as the intimate knowledge family members thought they had of one another. Survivors are left to wonder, "What made him do this to himself, and how did I, his sibling, fail him? Why him and not me?"

The stage of life you are in when a sibling commits suicide has a lot to do with the kind of pain you feel. The most vulnerable survivor of a sibling suicide is a child still living at home. She must struggle with her own grief about what her sibling has done when her parents are least able to help because of their own grief.

I Am Grieving Too

When Laura's brother was found dead by a self-inflicted bullet wound to his head, she felt as if she had lost a great deal more than a brother; she felt as if she had lost her whole family. Family and friends gathered around offering support to her mother and father, but no one paid much attention to fourteen-year-old Laura. Her mother was in deep despair. She could not speak to anyone. She cried, she screamed, and she seemed to Laura to be completely out of control and unavailable. Laura felt afraid of her and didn't know what to say to her. Anything she tried to talk about appeared to upset her mother even more, which was the last thing that Laura wanted to do. Her father, who had always been the one to whom Laura could turn most easily, didn't seem to know that she was there. Even in death her brother appeared to be getting more attention than she was.

Her own friends, young teenagers themselves, had little experience with death and less with suicide. In some ways they were afraid of what had happened to Laura's brother and also to Laura. Most found it impossible to talk with her about the fact that her brother had killed himself. They could manage a few words like "I'm so sorry" but then they wanted things to be back to normal. None could begin to empathize with Laura's feelings. Some of her closest friends began to withdraw from her, especially when she acted sad or depressed. Two of the girls in her class stopped speaking to her altogether. She learned from other friends that their families feared that Laura might be a bad influence on their daughters; they believed that she must come from some kind of bad family in which things like suicide could happen.

At home things were not improving either. Her mother remained deeply depressed. She stayed in her room crying almost all of the time. There had not been a meal prepared since her brother's death. The only time the house was cleaned at all was if Laura chose to do it. Her father was always either worried about her mother or involved in his own grieving process. All he would speak about was his dead son, wondering constantly why he had taken his own life. He never came up with an answer.

Laura's feelings were very confused. There didn't seem to be anyone to whom she could turn for comfort. Everyone around her was too wrapped up in pain. Laura felt great sadness about what her brother had done and great anger at him as well. He had always seemed to be both troubled and causing trouble at home. Her parents were always more involved with him than they were with her. His triumphs seemed more important, his problems more pressing. She had loved her brother, but she resented him also. She felt that she who gave her parents so little trouble got little attention as a reward. Now that she was desperately needy, she was getting none at all. She felt hurt and angry and confused. The jealous feelings she had felt toward her brother, but which she had been able to control, resurfaced now and left her feeling guiltier than ever. How could she be so angry at someone who had been miserable enough to take his own life?

Laura reached her breaking point when her parents decided to endow a scholarship to memorialize her brother. They planned to present it each year at the high school graduation ceremony. At the presentation they would make a speech about her brother and how tragic it was that he had committed suicide. Laura exploded with anger. She screamed that her parents must have little concern for her feelings if they could expose the family pain in such a public way. She didn't want to keep reminding people that she was the girl whose brother had committed suicide.

At first her parents became angry in return. They felt she was being selfish. They believed that by presenting a scholarship and speaking openly about the suicide they might reach another young person before he or she took the same drastic step. Only through lots of discussion and tears on both sides did they begin to recognize that Laura was having a hard time too.

Laura's experience is shared by many siblings. Even adults who have suffered the loss of a sister or brother have expressed their resentment at being treated as if they were secondary mourners. One woman was hurt that her mother had received innumerable messages of condolence for her son's death, but she had not received any. "My brother had died, but no one seemed to consider that I had strong feelings too," she complained.

Other siblings have found that instead of being ignored their parents focus on them so much that they might envy Laura's isolation. When loss leaves a void, people make changes in an attempt to fill that emptiness, but for parents to expect the surviving siblings to take the place of, or to fill the emptiness left by, the one who committed suicide is clearly an impossible demand.

I Can't Fill
the Space He Left

Jed's day began and ended with his mother coming to him so they could talk some more about his nineteen-year-old brother who had jumped from the attic of the family home. "She wanted to review every detail of Sam's life," he complained. "She would be furious if I wasn't interested in doing this. My mother believed that if I didn't talk about Sam with her all the time that I would forget him or that I didn't care about my brother."

Jed did care about Sam but he didn't want to talk about him

all the time. He wanted to get on with his own life. He also saw that talking about the suicide always upset his mother and made her cry. Only fifteen years old himself, he was frightened at seeing the parent on whom he relied so terribly upset. He couldn't understand that she needed to cry; he only knew that he wanted it to stop so she could be herself again. Like Laura, Jed was angry that Sam occupied more of the family's emotional space than when he was alive. Just when Jed's parents wanted him to be closer to them, all he wanted to do was to get away from all this discussion about suicide and death.

Jed's parents also became extremely worried about everything he did and everywhere he went. At fifteen he had begun to take fairly appropriate steps at adolescent separation from the family. Prior to Sam's suicide, his parents had been comfortable with allowing him to do so. Now they watched his every move. Jed was a sensitive and intelligent young man who recognized that they had just lost one child and didn't want to risk losing another, but it still made life very difficult for him. He even began to have thoughts about killing himself! It was the only way he could see of getting away from his parents' intrusiveness. He secretly wondered if that was the reason his brother had committed suicide.

You Must Have Been Lousy Parents

All brothers and sisters wonder why their siblings took their own lives. Anger at parents is a common but frequently hidden sibling reaction to suicide. The survivors, sensing their parents' distress and guilt over the suicide, cannot bring themselves to discuss the mistakes they believe their parents made. In this way they perpetuate secrets and hidden resentments within the family. Parents can also lose credibility with the surviving siblings who may tell themselves, "Since my parents didn't do such a good job with my sister or brother, maybe I cannot trust the way they are dealing with me either."

Rebellion is another typcial response. A surviving sibling can make use of the parents' apparent failure to reject parental direction. Angry accusations can leave the surviving sibling feeling even more guilty than he may already feel. Thirteen-year-old Dirk became a discipline problem for his parents after his eighteen-year-old brother committed suicide. Before his brother's death he had been a very obedient child. Now he stayed away from home without letting anyone know where he was, began to have failing grades in his schoolwork for the first time, and was reported to be experimenting with alcohol. He demanded increasing sums of money from his parents, who in their vulnerable position were reluctant to deny him anything. At first his parents, still shocked and grieving over the suicide, barely noticed what was happening to Dirk.

When his father, who was the first to begin to recover, began to pay more attention to his younger son and began to expect him to behave more as he had before, he found that he could no longer influence his son as he once could. Dirk was disrespectful and, at times, really nasty to his father. In some ways his father, who felt guilty about his older son's suicide and no longer was sure of his own parenting ability, thought that he deserved his younger son's hostility. He was unwilling to confront Dirk and the situation steadily became worse. Dirk felt that he was out of control and began to believe that no one cared enough about him to try to really help him. Since his parents had never had this experience before, they really didn't understand what was going on.

At support group meetings Dirk's father heard other brothers and sisters discuss what they went through after suicides in their families. He began to understand what his son might be experiencing and what Dirk needed from him. He stopped worrying that if he criticized his son, Dirk would say, "What do you know—you told my brother that and he killed himself because of you." He was then more able to be an active father to his surviving son.

Even when Dirk did say the words that they had both been fearing, he was able to hear them and respond to his son's fear and rage rather than to his own guilt. Dirk was finally able to say what he was feeling. He discovered that although his father might even share some of the same feelings, he could still act like a father to him. When this happened, the family was well on the way to recovery.

The Overresponsible Sibling

Some brothers and sisters have very different reactions from the ones we have been discussing. If you have had a responsible, parental relationship to a brother or sister who commits suicide, your reaction will probably be more like a mother or father's than the sibling responses we have been discussing. You may even feel a great deal of anger at your parents for seeming to have let you take over the responsibilities that should have been theirs.

Liz always felt more like a mother than a sister to her younger brother. She believed, but was never told, that her mother had been an alcoholic when the children were quite young. Although she had stopped drinking, she never seemed able to make decisions or to take charge. Their father was frequently away attending to business. When he was at home he didn't like to be confronted with problems.

The job of raising her younger brother, Paul, fell mostly to Liz. The two were very close and Paul talked most things over with his sister until he became fifteen or sixteen, when he began to be more reticient about sharing things about himself with anyone. Liz began to have concerns about what was going on with her brother and suspected that something was seriously the matter. When she tried to talk to her mother and father about Paul, neither one was interested and they reassured her that Paul's behavior was typical of boys his age. She felt that, as usual, neither took an interest in their children's problems.

Liz was torn when she left home to go away to college. She

worried about being away from her brother. She felt as if she were abandoning him, yet she wanted to have a chance at a life for herself. Although it was a difficult decision, she chose to leave.

Two years later, when Paul committed suicide, Liz was overcome with guilt. She felt as if it were her fault for abandoning him by leaving home. She felt as if she should have known that something was wrong with him. She thought that she had known it but hadn't done enough to make others aware of it. She began, as many parents do, to search for explanations for Paul's behavior. She bitterly resented the sympathy and attention her parents received, since she felt that she was the one entitled to it. She felt she had failed her brother and in some indirect way had caused his suicide. While family and friends were reassuring and supportive to her parents, no one considered what Liz might be feeling, especially because she had been away from home for a while. Liz found some relief when she joined a support group where she could discuss her feelings and others sympathized with her. Even in the groups, she sometimes felt strange because she felt more like the other parents than like the other siblings.

Julie, too, felt she had become a mother to her little sister while her parents were embroiled in a bitter and lengthy divorce. She became the only one to whom Lillie could turn. Lillie had always been jealous of Julie's accomplishments and her apparent role as the oldest and favorite in the family. Julie is quite beautiful and had achieved success as a model and actress. Julie struggled to build Lillie's self-confidence while trying not to feel guilty that her own successes caused Lillie such anguish. She felt responsible for her sister but also resented her accusations and hostility.

When Lillie chose to take her own life, Julie's first feeling was a terrible raging anger that Lillie did this to her. After all Julie had done for her, how could she repay Julie in this way? Julie was afraid that Lillie meant to get back at her for seeming to be better than her little sister. Julie felt that she should have been able to give more to Lillie, even if it meant having less for herself. For a long time she stopped doing many of the things that had made Lillie jealous. She wore only old, unattractive clothing and no makeup. She would not apply for modeling jobs or attend auditions. It was many months before she could see that this was not going to help her sister now and it never would have.

Parenting Your Parents

Many brothers and sisters of a suicide victim become worried about their parents' ability to survive this kind of trauma. It is not uncommon for some to become overly concerned about their parents' well-being. These siblings may be putting aside their own needs to attend to those of their parents. They assume a parental role toward their own parents. Those who have formerly been like parents to their siblings are especially prone to do this.

When Clara's brother committed suicide, the family was deeply shocked. He had been a charismatic and much admired young man. He seemed successful at almost everything he did. Perhaps this was why he could not recover from the single failure he had known. No one could understand it, least of all Clara, who had always been content to bask in the glory of her younger brother. When he died, she had been planning to be married. She immediately canceled her engagement and moved back into her parents' home and took over many aspects of their lives. Her father was too depressed to run his business effectively, so Clara did that. Her mother couldn't manage the household, so she did that also. She spent all of her free time with her parents.

Clara's fiancé hung around for a while, but eventually their relationship ended. Clara was sure that her parents would never survive the tragedy of her brother's death without her. She was sure that if she were to separate from them, they could not go on living.

We urge you to share your feelings with others and to invite them to open up to you. If your parents are really not available to you at this time, you would be wise to seek counseling from a reliable professional. If you are a student, your guidance counselor or school psychologist can probably help you to find appropriate help.

Chapter 12

Support:
You Are Not
Alone

When someone you love commits suicide you feel abandoned and alone. You believe something that feels this bad cannot possibly have been experienced by anyone else. You feel set apart. It is frightening to feel this way and makes it difficult to recover.

Many Have Come Before You

As you have realized in this book, statistically you are not alone. At least a quarter of a million people a year become survivors of the suicide of a loved one.

You may wonder why you have never encountered another survivor if there are so many. They, like you, may have been afraid to share their grief because of shame and guilt. Until very recently suicide was not discussed openly. Many survivors have told us that even they didn't know until years later that the death of a loved one had been a suicide.

Today survivors recognize the benefits of sharing their painful experiences with others, making it possible for those who had once been isolated to experience the relief of sharing their burden. Mary's mother committed suicide twenty years before Mary found her way to a support group meeting. She spent her first meeting listening intently while her tears flowed throughout the session. Finally someone asked her why she was crying since surely she had finished mourning her mother's death many years ago. Mary answered that she was crying for herself because this was the first time since her mother's suicide that she had met anyone else who shared her painful experience. "I have always thought of myself as different and despicable because my mother could take her own life and leave me behind. I was the only person I ever knew to whom this had happened. I believe that meeting all of you will change my life."

You Are Not So Different

Finding out that you are not alone is one kind of support. It is important for you to know that no matter what has happened to you, no matter how terrible, no matter how unimaginable, it has happened to someone else also. It is essential to remember the words of the psychotherapist, Harry Stack Sullivan, who observed that, "We are all more simply human than otherwise." We urge you to find a support group so that you can meet others who have had a similar experience. We believe that sharing with other survivors of suicide, rather than those bereaved from other causes, is important. Many of the survivors we have met have attended other bereavement groups and have not found them as helpful.

Frequently survivors found that, either openly or subtly, others made them feel unwelcome. Survivors have reported that other mourners seemed to believe that since the losses they were grieving were losses by "choice," they were not true mourners. Worse, they felt they were somehow responsible for the choice their loved one had made.

There are no such biases in suicide survivor groups. One of the healing aspects of being in such a group is when you meet other survivors you find they are no different than anyone else. They are mothers, fathers, sisters, brothers, husbands, wives, and sons and daughters who have lost someone they loved very much. They are not marked or tarnished or remarkable in any way but that they are suffering from a hurtful loss. When you meet them you will see that you are not so different.

Dorothea had been a quiet and self-effacing woman. She was a devoted but insecure mother who tried her best, got advice when she felt she needed it, but never felt confident that she knew what was best, especially for her oldest son, Stuart, who usually seemed to be having one problem or another. He had learning difficulties from the time he was in second grade. In high school he became a heavy drinker who sometimes used illegal drugs as well, probably in an unsuccessful effort to escape from his academic problems.

Dorothea's husband died when her boys were eleven and eight years old. Her problems with Stuart became more difficult at that time. She arranged for psychotherapy for Stuart and for herself, but it did not make lasting changes in Stuart's life. When his downward spiral ended in suicide, Dorothea was convinced it had been her fault. She suffered from the would have's and should have's, the endless feelings of guilt and self-recrimination. Even the fact that her second son, Gary, had a successful life was not enough to break her conviction that she was worthless. Stuart's suicide was all the proof she needed.

When she attended a survivor group and met other parents, she was amazed. Among those in the room the first night she attended were an elegantly dressed physician who spoke eloquently about her daughter's suicide; a teacher whose son had committed suicide despite having devoted parents who had supported him in whatever he had wanted to do; a mother who had returned to school to study family counseling after her son's suicide so that she could be useful to others with family problems; and a father of eight who had lost one son to suicide but whose seven other children, several of whom had come to the group with him, were well adjusted and productive young people. Dorothea remarked, "Just meeting these other parents whose children have committed suicide and finding that they are caring, loving people made me feel that perhaps I might not be such a monster either."

Dorothea had been reluctant to come to a group where she would meet other survivors. Who were these people who had lost loved ones to suicide? She, like so many others, made the false assumption that they must be bad people if their loved ones chose death as an escape.

From her first meeting she learned how wrong her assumption had been. No one she met had not cared about the person he or she lost. She quickly came to see her belief that survivors must be of a different sort was unfounded. By getting to know other survivors, you will see that you are not so different.

What Is a Support Group?

You may be wondering just what happens at a support group. We have noticed that many things go on at support groups. Some of what takes place is part of the plan and some of the best things that happen may not have been planned.

On a typical Thursday night the members of Ann's group begin to gather before she arrives. If there is someone new, the others quickly introduce themselves and make him or her feel welcome. Older members remember how frightened they were when they were new. They feel a desire to integrate a newcomer into the group and to help that person because it reinforces the fact that they are healing too.

Formal introductions take place when the meeting officially begins. Each participant is asked to state his or her name and what brought them to the group. You may make a longer statement at this point if you wish. You may use your entire name or just your first name. We do not insist on anonymity because we do not believe that there is any reason to hide that you are the survivor of suicide. However, if anyone wishes to conceal his full name, he is free to do so.

By the time we have gone once around the room and each person has stated whose suicide they have come to recover from, there is an intense bonding in the room. Just being in the presence of so many others who are sharing the feelings you believed you alone suffered has the power to begin the healing process. At this time anyone may take the floor and speak about whatever is on his or her mind. A free exchange of ideas and feelings begins and continues for the rest of the meeting. The only rule is that just one person speaks at a time. Often this is a hard rule to follow as emotions are stirred up and everyone wants to express himself at once.

Members often speak about where they are in the healing process. Tears are common but surprisingly so is laughter. Every emotion is expressed at one time or another. Often the most important exchanges occur between new members, who come feeling despair and hopelessness, and older members, who recall they once felt the same way. The older member remembers how it once was for him and is astonished to find that he is in a different place in his life; he never thought this could happen. The newer member finds it hard to believe she will ever achieve what the others have but gains some hope that it might be so.

Telling stories occupies a good deal of time in the meetings. Members gain strength from sharing stories. When you are able to use your story to bring insight and hope to someone else, you begin to believe that something good can come from your loss and pain. The terrible experience that you would never have chosen to have can at least be helpful to a fellow sufferer. That is, perhaps, the greatest value that comes from participation in a support group.

After the formal part of the meeting is over, even those members who have had little to say during the meeting seem to become talkative as the group moves out of the building. Sometimes folks remain in the parking lot talking for a long time. Phone numbers are exchanged with offers to be available if others want to talk before the next meeting time. Friendships begin based on bonds of mutual pain. From the ashes of disaster new relationships tentatively flower as people begin to regain a sense of self-worth.

Starting Your Own Group

This book with its survivor stories is a substitute for a group if none exists in your area. Perhaps after meeting the survivors we have introduced to you in these pages you will gain the desire and courage to find a way to meet other survivors in person. One way might be to contact your local mental health clinic or association to see if it might have an interest in forming a survivor group. Advertising for other survivors is another way. When this has been tried, the numbers of survivors who appear is astonishing. Those recently bereaved as well as those who have been secretly struggling with a suicide in their past come to find the solace that a group experience can bring.

All you really need to start a support group is a meeting place and participants. Many support groups around the country have been formed by survivors for survivors and function quite well without professional leadership. We do not wish to detract from their work in any way. We do believe that something can be added by having a mental health professional facilitate the work of the group.

Suicide does not occur in a vacuum. It usually follows a period of turmoil. Survivors are often in states of heightened emotional distress prior to the suicide, which adds additional stresses. This kind of pressure can exacerbate tendencies to emotional instability that may already exist. Although a support group can be helpful, you may also need additional therapeutic intervention to help you through this trying time. A professional can help to make that assessment and guide you to the proper treatment. A trained professional can also help the group discussion along, making sure that all have a chance to be heard, and drawing out those who may need some encouragement to share their feelings.

We have found that very often survivors are disappointed and angry at mental health professionals. Most of your loved ones had had contact with psychiatrists, psychologists, or social workers at one time or another prior to the suicide. You may believe that a professional was not helpful in preventing the suicide. You may be reluctant to seek the help of a mental health professional now, wondering how she can help you any better than she helped the one you loved and lost.

Even if you are in need of counseling for yourself, you may hesitate to obtain it. You may be willing, however, to attend a support group like the ones we have described. If a mental health professional is the facilitator, you will begin to form a relationship that may help you to regain some confidence in a field you believe has failed you before.

Sharing and Caring

Speaking to others is an important way to recover from any traumatic experience. Usually the people in your family or your close friends are the ones who provide support. In fact, experts say that your ability to successfully recover from a traumatic shock can be predicted by evaluating the strength of your support system.

Unfortunately, when someone you are close to commits suicide, it is likely that this death will also be traumatic to most of the people who comprise your support network. All of you will need others to lean on and none of you will be able to provide much support for anyone else. When one member of a family wants to talk all the time, while another needs to withdraw and to not listen to the other's pain, there is not much room for the kind of support that leads to healing. One member of a family may be identified as needy, while another takes the role of the helper, neglecting his own needs. Another scenario is that members of a family turn against one another in disappointment because they are not getting the nurturance they need. Frustration at being deprived of a nurturing supporter leads to anger. Every member of the family is suffering and wants to be taken care of, not to serve as a caretaker, at this time.

One of your strongest needs will be to tell your story repeatedly. Those who know you well, even your closest friends, will tire of hearing you long before you are tired of repeating yourself. Telling your story is your way of trying to understand and incorporate this horror into your life. It will take a long time.

Your friends, even those who care the most and have only your well-being at heart, will soon encourage you to put the past behind you. They will tell you it has been three months or six months or whatever arbitrary time limit they believe is appropriate for you to suffer, and it is now time to be over it, but you will go on believing you will never be over it. They are not completely wrong. Mourning is a finite process. One day mourning will no longer consume all of your life. However, the length of mourning is up to you, not some preconceived notion that someone else may have.

Your family and friends have another reason for wanting you to be your old self again. They miss you. At one time you were able to be attuned to their needs and concerns, not just your own. You were available to hear their stories, to be supportive of them. You could have fun, do a favor, share a task with them, or do whatever it was that brought you together and kept you involved with one another. For them, you have also become a casualty of suicide. You may begin to see these people as uncaring and unsympathetic. They are probably just overburdened.

These are the reasons that it is important to engage supports outside of your usual circle at this time. Members of survivor support groups know that you need a place where you are free to tell your story and share your pain as often as you choose. All that is required is that you give the other group members the same chance. You will find strength from hearing the stories of others, and you will find that your tragedy enables you to be helpful to others who are in similar pain.

When a Support Group Is Not Enough

We have said many times that we do not put a limit on the amount of time it will take you to recover from the suicide of a loved one. Nevertheless, we find that sometimes it seems to be taking too long. This is especially true when nothing seems to be changing for you at all. You have chosen "survivor of suicide" as your identity and seem content to remain in that role. You appear to have given up aspirations to do anything else in your life. Even after a great deal of time has passed, you are unable to see value in anything in your life.

When this occurs, we believe that something else is going on for you. Unresolved feelings about other personal conflicts have become intertwined with feelings about the suicide. This phenomenon is not exclusively a problem of survivor groups but is present whenever someone tries to account for all the problems in his life because he is suffering from one malady. Whenever we try to attribute all of life's problems to a single cause, we lose sight of how complex our lives really are. A suicide of a loved one occurs in the life of someone who already has a personality and means of coping with conflicts and problems. A survivor has relationships and a way of life that predate the suicide and continue during and after recovery.

Sometimes survivors try to excuse themselves from paying attention to other issues because they are so consumed by the trauma of suicide. We have, for example, seen survival issues used to cover up failing marriages or as masks for social phobias. The trauma of losing someone to suicide, as difficult as that may be, gets used as an excuse for not coping with other problems. That is a time when a professional group leader could interevene to suggest that you pay attention to the hidden issues. A fellow group member might see this just as clearly but may hesitate to tell you, believing that you are in a group for support, not to be confronted with other problems.

Mark lost his fiancée to suicide just a few months before they were to be married. He was an attractive twenty-eight-year-old when he first came to a survivor group, deeply depressed over the loss of Linda. "Nothing," he said, "will ever mean anything to me again." For many years nothing did. At first, it was not surprising that Mark did little else but go to work and attend his support group. After one year in the group it began to seem odd, especially as others were moving ahead while he kept saying the same things over and over. After two years with no change, it was clear that Mark's problem was more than one of being a survivor of suicide.

Whenever the leader or other group members confronted Mark about anything in his life other than Linda's suicide, he would reiterate that nothing else mattered and how could anyone expect that anything else ever would. He was adamant about not risking having another girlfriend, or in fact, any friend at all. Gradually it became clear that Mark had never had a relationship with any other woman. He had never had a friend outside of his workplace. Even when he was younger, he had been very socially isolated. Linda had pursued him and had always been the aggressor in their relationship; otherwise he would not have become involved with her.

Mark had a characterological problem. He had been socially isolated for all of his life. He had been seen as strange by others because of his aloofness. Linda's suicide became an acceptable rationalization for why he was alone. It was not really the reason, but it was an excuse that people did not seem to question.

Mark eventually agreed to speak privately with the group's

facilitator, a professional social worker. He finally admitted to his lifelong difficulties and his dissatisfaction with how limited his life was. He had liked having a girlfriend very much. When he was with Linda he had felt so much more a part of life. They did things together. He didn't have to be alone all the time. He wanted to be part of life again, but he was afraid.

The leader referred Mark to an individual therapist. Mark never spoke in the group about what went on in those sessions, but he did begin to speak of doing other things in his life besides watching television alone in his apartment after work. After another year he announced that he would not be coming to the group any longer. He no longer wished to center his life around being a survivor of suicide but planned to pursue other activities. He shyly said that he was seeing a new woman and was ready to give up ruminating about Linda. Coming to the group made him focus on Linda and he was now ready to stop. Linda would always be an important part of his history, but he was now more interested in his future than in his past.

Chapter 13

Healing:
Moving Ahead

Healing, ultimately, is what this book is all about. The old adage, "Time heals all wounds," is not necessarily true for survivors of suicide. Time is necessary for healing, but time alone is not enough. We see ample evidence of this from survivors who come seeking help five, ten, even twenty or more years after the suicide has taken place. Many are individuals who have kept the suicide a secret, treating it as a taboo subject.

Healing the pain of a loved one's suicide requires sharing with other survivors through a support group or through reading a book like this, as well as sharing with other family members and friends. Buried feelings fester. Shared feelings enrich and lead to growth and healing.

There are as many paths to healing as there are those who are hurting. Each one takes a different direction. Some appear to be direct roads; others twist and turn. Some traverse level territory; others pass through valleys and peaks. No one way is correct for everyone. You will take the journey that you need to take. Do not expect it to be easy. Do not expect the trip to be quick. You will lose many things along the way: preconceived ideas, old ways of thinking, notions about explanations, guilt, and retribution. You will gain many others: sensitivity, understanding, compassion, and forgiveness of yourself and others.

You Will Never Know Why

The expectation that you can find an explanation for a suicide is one of the first things you must give up on your road to healing. Most of us believe if we try hard enough we can understand almost anything. We would like to be able to do so because, if we could, perhaps we could also control things and make them turn out the way we want. Early in the grieving process, while you are still looking for peace through denial, you unreasonably believe that if you could understand why the suicide occurred you might be able to turn back time and make it all turn out differently. You could recapture the moment of fateful decision and reverse the dreadful results. You might want to change how you spent the last few hours of your loved one's life or your entire relationship with him. Of course, even if you could discern the reason for the suicide, you could not change one minute of the past. One day you will come to terms with the fact that you will never know what led to suicide, nor can you now change anything that preceded it.

Many survivors spend much time and energy reconstructing the last days and hours of the life of their loved one. It is as if they believe that in the final events of life an explanation for suicide will become apparent. Some even find what look like precipitating events such as disappointments, disillusions, losses, humiliations, and fears. No one has yet discovered, however, anything unique, anything that many others have not faced as part of life and come through without committing suicide. Some survivors also reflect on entire lives for explanations of the tragic ending. They, too, find conflicts, problems, troubles of all kinds in the lives of their loved one, but none of these is unique to those who chose suicide.

There will come a day when you will admit to yourself that you will probably never find a satisfactory explanation. More importantly you will realize that, even if you could find that explanation, nothing would change; your loved one would still not be alive. There is nothing you can do now to change that sad fact. Once you are able to stop believing that anything can undo what has happened, you are beginning to heal. Now you will be able to grieve, to miss your loved one, to find a way to fill the empty space her death has left. You will no longer be distracted from this task by ruminative questions of why this came to be. As you let go of trying to find explanations, trying to assign causality and blame, you also let go of guilty self-recriminations.

Healing from a loss by suicide is a complex process. First you must come to terms with the fact of suicide. Once you have accomplished that, you must still grieve.

Grieving Is Not Loving

That grieving is not equivalent to loving is not an original idea nor does it pertain uniquely to survivors of suicide. Many survivors believe that while they are grieving for their lost one, they are proving how much love they felt for him. You may believe if you give up being in pain, if you have a comfortable moment, if you laugh or find some enjoyment, that this behavior is a betrayal of your loved one. You may believe that all your memories of him must be accompanied by sadness.

Nothing is further from the truth. You have many memories of your loved one. The time you had with him can be remembered with joy as well as with sadness. Of course you feel sad that he is no longer with you, but you can also remember with gladness the times you did have together.

Andrew loved his young wife passionately. He recalled that they had shared moments of great happiness as well as those of intense pain during the years they spent together. After her suicide, which he never came to understand, Andrew felt he had to devote his life to mourning her death. He believed that only by remaining depressed could he be true to her memory. He believed that to feel any other way was a betrayal of the love he had for her. Even memories of the happy times they shared had to be experienced with pain because she was no longer with him.

Whenever Andrew began to feel "better," he would remind himself that he had no right to feel relief and he would dredge up some more bad feelings. Whenever he realized that he had not thought about his wife for a while, he made himself do so. He came to see that he was operating as if the depth of his depression was proof that he loved his wife and could not be blamed for her death, by himself or anyone else.

Once he realized that this was his assumption, he recognized what we have been saying, that grieving is not tantamount to loving. He was still alive. He was not the one who had made the choice to abandon life and loved ones. Andrew was able to make the choice of being alive. He knew that it was now his choice to give up constant pain. Sometimes pain still comes. Andrew accepts it when it hits him. Sometimes he even welcomes it because it reminds him of his wife, but he no longer actively seeks it. When he laughs or smiles or takes pleasure in something that happens in his life, he no longer feels ashamed. There are times when pain comes and he makes an active choice to fight it rather than to succumb to it. He feels that he is entitled to create a new life for himself. Accepting that grieving is not the same as loving, Andrew has begun to heal.

Writing About It

Writing out your thoughts is an excellent way to get in touch with what you are feeling inside. Undistracted by the need to communicate with anyone but yourself, uninfluenced by another's response, your uncensored feelings can emerge. Although we have been stressing the value of sharing, we also encourage you to have private times with your own thoughts after the suicide. Many find that after they put troubling feelings on paper they are freer to have other feelings and think other thoughts. By having made a record of what you are feeling, it is as if you no longer have to ruminate or continue to replay these feelings in your head. When the feelings are down on paper they belong to you whether you are actively thinking about them or not.

After a sudden death there often remains unfinished business between you and your deceased loved one, words you never said, conflicts between you that are unresolved. Telling her in writing is a way to communicate your feelings so they do not remain locked within you. Survivors have been known to write letters and burn them to send their message or to leave them at graves or other significant places. These communications can provide you with the sense of closure that is not present after a sudden death.

You may find that poetry is your way of speaking your feelings. Many survivors have found this to be true. The newsletters of survivor groups frequently contain poems written by members. Often people who have never been moved to express themselves through the written word before find they have become eloquent writers.

Others have written biographical remembrances of their loved one. This can be a way of immortalizing her. You may find that by putting your memories on paper your mind will become more peaceful. No longer are you afraid that something will be forgotten. Writing your loved one's story helps you to make sense of her life.

Reading

Many survivors find solace in reading all they can find about suicide. Although you will never know what it was that led your loved one to commit suicide, you may find peace in gaining the greatest intellectual understanding that you can about the phenomenon of suicide. Knowledge may help you conclude that you did all there was to do. It may relieve you of tortured questioning about what you missed or might have done differently. Many believe that by acquiring extensive knowledge about suicide they can be assured that they will never miss known precursors of suicidal ideation in someone else they care about.

Many survivors say they cannot understand what leads someone to the decision to commit suicide. Reading can help you to be more empathetic with the state of mind of someone when he makes the decision to take his own life. We have included a selection of books in the Suggested Readings section.

Helping Others:
Using What You Know

As your pain subsides, and it will, you will find that you have learned a great many things. You now know more about suicide, what comes before it, what comes after it, and how its side effects touch the lives of its survivors for years to come. Through the introspection that accompanies mourning, through contemplation and observation, you have gradually become a student of suicidology. Many survivors find that sharing what they have learned is important to their healing.

A major premise of the self-help movement (which includes survivor groups) is that by sharing your story, experiences, hope, and strength with others, you can reinforce your own growth and healing. When you are going through a difficult time, it may seem that you are not making any progress. One day seems like the one that came before it with no respite in sight. When you speak with someone who is newer to the journey than you are, you can see how far you really have come. You are making progress after all. If you can see that you have already made some changes, then you can believe that continued growth is possible.

Paula sometimes smiles these days, but she certainly didn't when she first came to a survivor group two weeks after her husband committed suicide. She says she doesn't feel any different than she did a year ago, but when Eva recently joined the group after her husband's suicide Paula could see the difference between them. She was able to see the changes she had made by comparing herself to Eva. More than that, she identified with what Eva was feeling. She told her what had happened to her, how she had spent most of her time crying too. Paula told Eva that she had not been able to go out of the house and that she had been barely able to get out of bed. As she recalled her story, she could see that she no longer was the way she had been. As she tried to help Eva believe that her feelings, too, would change, she clearly recognized that her own had. Paula felt good about sharing with Eva. She came to believe that, if by sharing her experience she could help another person toward recovery, her own tragedy had not been meaningless.

Some survivors have helped themselves and others by starting survivor support groups where none exist. Survivor groups originated not with mental health professionals but with survivors themselves reaching out to other sufferers. These pioneers had the intuition that they needed to share with those with similar experiences in order to heal themselves. They simultaneously provided a much-needed service for others. Some survivors use their newfound knowledge to prevent others from choosing suicide. Suicide hot lines provide a troubled person with someone to speak with. Frequently many staff members are survivors of suicide. They are interested in using what they have learned to counsel others who are in crisis or jeopardy. Their own stories and heightened sensitivities become tools for reaching out to others. The survivors take solace from the knowledge that their sad experience has had some use in saving another from the fate of their loved one. Pain has borne the fruit of loving service.

Teaching and disseminating information about the warning signals of suicide is another area in which survivors have found themselves useful. Some have volunteered to serve on state or local committees for suicide prevention. Many have chosen to go public with their stories in order to educate the public about the danger signs of suicide.

Milton had always been rather shy. The suicide of his only son at age twenty, alone and far from home, seemed like one more tragic blow in a life filled with failed opportunities and disappointments. All suicides are tragic, but this one seemed especially so since it was apparent that the young man was trying to get help at the time, but his signals regarding his suicidal intention had been missed. Milton believed that had they been better understood, his son might still be alive.

Milton had never spoken up much before. You probably would not have noticed him in a room with other people, nor would he have tried to make you do so. All that changed after his son's death. He wanted to make sure that no one again missed masked pleas for help from someone who was considering suicide. He contacted the media, his congressman, his senators, and the local board of education. It became his life purpose to let everyone know how crucial it is that suicidal people be recognized and helped. He disseminated literature about the warning signs of suicide to school principals and workers in health clinics. He spoke on radio and appeared on TV shows whenever he could get himself invited. Milton could not bring his own son back to life, but he could give meaning to his son's death by trying to save others like him. Milton might have lived out the rest of his life in quiet despair, but he chose to be someone who made a difference while also helping himself to heal.

Mental health workers have often been attracted to the profession by their own experiences. Some survivors decide to enter the mental health field as a way of helping others. They bring their experience to their work. The awareness that the end product of mental distress can be suicide helps make them responsible, caring practitioners. If you choose this path, you must also learn that your experience with suicide has taught you about just one path that people with problems may take. Through academic training and supervised work experiences you will learn about the many varieties of mental and emotional distress and how to intervene to alleviate pain.

You probably have strong feelings about how the news of your loved one's suicide was handled by the media. You have also become highly sensitized to how other suicides are reported. You may even believe that the reporting of another suicide led indirectly to the suicide of your own loved one through what is known as the *contagion effect*.

There are two kinds of stories about suicides that may influence others to take their own lives. One is the kind of story that makes the life of the suicide victim seem glamorous. Though his life ends in tragedy, it is portrayed in such a way as to seem especially admirable and worthy of envy from others. His death is reported as being followed by a great outpouring of love from friends and family. The victim becomes a tragic hero. Little or no mention is made of the troubles that led to his choice of death over life. No one writes about the ongoing grief and dislocation that will be felt by the survivors for a long time after the death. To a person feeling depressed and alone, all the attention and glamor following suicide may make it seem like an attractive alternative to hopelessness and despair.

The other aspect of reporting that may be found objectionable is the detailed coverage of the method chosen for committing suicide. These articles can read like "how to" manuals for anyone contemplating a similar act. Some survivors have chosen to make use of what they know by writing to the media every time an article about a suicide appears and commenting on how it was handled. They hope to educate reporters and editors about the effect of their words on the public.

Memorials

After a death many people wish to make financial contributions in memory of the deceased. Making use of such offerings to create a memorial in honor of your loved one is another way of creating something positive out of something painful. Some survivors have endowed scholarships in the name of the person whom they lost. The scholarship can be for a student who is overcoming emotional problems, for a person pursuing suicidology as a career, or for any reason you deem worthwhile whether it is related to suicide prevention or not.

One family created a scholarship to be awarded at the graduation ceremonies of the high school from which their son had graduated a few years before. He had not been a particularly good student and struggled throughout high school. There had been little recognition that he was a learning-disabled youngster. Having a learning disability is one of the risk factors for suicide.

After his death, his family came to believe that perhaps if he had had more recognition for what he was able to achieve, in spite of his disability, he might have had more confidence in himself and might still be alive. If they could not give that recognition to their own son, they could give it to other young people. The scholarship was to be awarded to the student who showed the most improvement in his senior year in high school.

These parents attend graduation ceremonies every year to present the award themselves. They have yet to be able to do so without struggling through their own tears as they speak about their dead son and why they are presenting this award. While remembering their own son they offer hope and strength to another struggling young person.

Another scholarship endowed to memorialize a child's suicide is given to a person studying special education by the parents of a young woman who took her own life in her thirties. Special education was their daughter's profession. They believe that she had chosen to help children having emotional difficulties with the learning process because she, too, had had emotional struggles. She tried to use her own experience to make life easier and better for others. She eventually took her own life, perhaps because her struggles were too great and maybe because there had not been a caring person available to help at the moment she needed it. Her parents endowed a scholarship so that someone would be there for another child in need.

These are some examples of the things that others have done to create something positive from their tragedy. The ultimate phase in the healing process comes when you are able to acknowledge what you have learned through your suffering. When you are able to stop thinking mainly about yourself and what has happened to you, and can think about what you can do for others, then you will know you are truly healing.

Some Final Thoughts

We hope a time comes for you, as it has for others, when you are able to accept your loved one's suicide as having been his own choice. We hope you can believe he made that choice because he felt that it was the only one left to him, the only way he knew to solve his problems. Even as your rational mind loudly protests that he used a permanent solution to a temporary problem, you can accept that he was convinced it was the best way out.

Whatever your beliefs are about afterlife, you probably believe that death brings relief from pain and suffering for the person who dies, if not for his loved ones. To help you comprehend how a tormented mind may long for the peace that death can bring, we leave you with the words of the poet Algernon Swinburne:

From too much love of living
From hope and fear set free,
We thank with brief thanksgiving
Whatever Gods may be
That no life lives forever
That dead men rise up never;
That even the weariest river
Winds somewhere safe to sea.

Suggested Readings

Alvarez, A. *The Savage God: A Study of Suicide*. New York: Random House, 1972.

Barrett, Terrence. *Life After Suicide: The Survivor's Grief Experience*. Fargo: Richtman's Printing, 1989.

Bolton, I. *My Son . . . My Son . . . : A Guide to Healing After Death, Loss, or Suicide*. Atlanta: The Bolton Press, 1983.

Cain, A. (ed.). *Survivors of Suicide*. Springfield: C. C. Thomas, 1972.

Chance, Sue. *Stronger Than Death*. New York, W. W. Norton, 1992.

Colt, George Howe. *The Enigma of Suicide*. New York: Summit Books, 1991.

Dunne, E. J. (ed.). *Suicide and Its Aftermath*. New York: W. W. Norton, 1987.

Hewett, J. H. *After Suicide*. Philadelphia: Westminster Press, 1980.

Klagsbrun, F. *Too Young to Die*. New York: Pocket Books, 1981.

Lukas, C., and Seiden, H. *Silent Grief*. New York: Charles Scribner's Sons, 1987.

Maris, Ronald. *Pathways to Suicide*. Baltimore: Johns Hopkins University Press, 1981.

Robinson, R. *Survivors of Suicide*. Santa Monica: IBS Press, 1989.

Wallace, S. *After Suicide*. New York: Wiley, 1973.

Wass, H., and Corr, C. A. (eds.). *Helping Children Cope with Death: Guidelines and Resources*. New York: Hemisphere Publishing Corporation, 1982.

Appendix:
Support Group Directory

This directory was compiled by the American Association of Suicidology and is printed here with their permission.

The American Association of Suicidology (AAS) compiled this directory from a variety of sources and does not guarantee the accuracy, reliability, or completeness of this information. Neither AAS nor the authors of this book have undertaken any independent review or examination of the individuals or organizations listed. Both AAS and the authors specifically disclaim any liability or responsibility for any actions or statements by any of the organizations or individuals listed. All information and statements contained in this directory are provided by and the responsibility of the individuals or organizations who have provided the information or statements to AAS. Publication in this directory does not imply any opinion, endorsement, or approval by AAS, its officers or members, or by the authors or publishers of this book. The directory is offered for information and reference only.

Suggested Groups

Support Group Leadership
Peer—Peer facilitated
Prof—Mental health professional facilitated
P/P—Combination peer and professional facilitation

Charge for Service
Yes—Fee charged for service
No—No fee charged for service

Alabama

BIRMINGHAM
Mental Health Association Central Alabama
Crisis Center, Inc.
Linda Cordisco
3600 8th Ave. S., Ste. 501
Birmingham, AL 35222
(205) 323-7782
Leadership: P/P
Charge: No

Alaska

FAIRBANKS
Fairbanks Crisis Line
P.O. Box 70908
Fairbanks, AK 99707
(907) 451-8600
Leadership: P/P
Charge: No

Alberta

CALGARY
Canadian Mental Health Association Suicide Services
Mary Canning
723 14th St. NW, #103
Calgary, AB T2N 2A4
Canada
(403) 297-1700
Leadership: Prof
Charge: No

CALGARY
Fellowship of Suicide Survivors (Calgary)
Ruth Lehman
40 Carnarvon Way NW
Calgary, AB T2K 1W4
Canada
(403) 289-0825

(403) 228-7943 Doreen Grant
Leadership: Peer
Charge: Yes

EDMONTON
L.O.S.S.
Ollie Schulz
13308 91 St.
Edmonton, AB T5E 3P8
Canada
(403) 476-7035
Leadership: Peer
Charge: No

EDMONTON
Suicide Bereavement
Community Connections
Brenda Simon
202-10534 124 St.
Edmonton, AB T5N 1S1
Canada
(403) 482-0198
(403) 482-4636
Leadership: P/P
Charge: No

FORT MCMURRAY
Some Other Solutions Society
  for Crisis Prevention
Keltie Paul
500-208 Beacon Hill Dr.
Fort McMurray, AB T9H 2R1
Canada
(403) 743-8605
Leadership: P/P
Charge: No

Arizona

TEMPE
Survivors of Suicide Groups &
  Prevention Programs
EMPACT—Suicide Prevention
  Center
Judith Lewis
1232 E. Broadway Rd., Ste. 120
Tempe, AZ 85282
(602) 784-1514
Leadership: P/P
Charge: No

TUCSON
Survivors of Suicide
Help on Call Crisis Line
Vicky Stromee
P.O. Box 43696
Tucson, AZ 85733
(602) 323-9373
Leadership: P/P
Charge: No

YUMA
Survivors of Suicide
Sandy Conrad
P.O. Box 4201
Yuma, AZ 85366
(602) 783-1860
Leadership: P/P
Charge: No

British Columbia

NANAIMO
Survivors of Suicide
Mary Barker
4944 Rutherford Rd.

Nanaimo, BC V9T 5P1
Canada
(604) 758-3190
Leadership: Peer
Charge: No

VANCOUVER
S.A.F.E.R.
Linda Rosenfeld
300, 2425 Quebec St.
Vancouver, BC V5T 4L6
Canada
(604) 879-9251
Leadership: Prof
Charge: No

California

BERKELEY
Grief Counseling Program
Suicide Prevention/Crisis Intervention of Alameda County
Karen Newcomb
P.O. Box 9102
Berkeley, CA 94709
(510) 889-1104
(510) 848-1515
Leadership: P/P
Charge: Yes

BURLINGAME
Crisis Intervention & Suicide
   Prevention Center
1811 Trousdale Dr.
Burlingame, CA 94010
(415) 692-6662
Leadership: Prof
Charge: Yes

CASTRO VALLEY
Grief Counseling Program
Suicide & Crisis Services of Alameda County
Karen Newcomb
21636 Redwood Rd.
Castro Valley, CA 94546
(510) 889-1104
Leadership: Prof
Charge: Yes

CHICO
Suicide Survivors Bereavement
   Group
Butte County Mental Health
Patty Krause
592 Rio Lindo
Chico, CA 95926
(916) 891-2832
Leadership: Peer
Charge: No

DAVIS
Spring Group/Fall Group
Suicide Prevention of Yolo
   County
Diane Sommers
P.O. Box 622
Davis, CA 95617
(916) 756-7542
Leadership: Prof
Charge: No

FRESNO
Help in Emotional Trouble
Mary Cardell
P.O. Box 4282
Fresno, CA 93744
(209) 486-4703

Leadership: Peer
Charge: No

FRESNO
Survivors of Suicide
Dick & Sandy Gallagher
1092 E. Sierra St.
Fresno, CA 93710
(209) 431-8994
(209) 299-0457
Leadership: Peer
Charge: No

GARDEN GROVE
Crystal Cathedral
S.O.S./Survivors of Suicide
Jeri Livingstone
12141 Lewis Ave.
Garden Grove, CA 92644
(714) 971-4129
(714) 539-1429
Leadership: Peer
Charge: No

JACKSON
New Horizons
Anne Skaggs
Daneri Mortuary
415 Broadway
Jackson, CA 95642
(209) 223-0793
Leadership: P/P
Charge: No

LOS ANGELES
Suicide Support Group
Jonathan Gilbert Jacoves Memo-
rial Fund
Jeanne Jacoves

University of Judaism
15600 Mulholland
Los Angeles, CA 90077
(310) 476-9777
(213) 934-7958
Leadership: P/P
Charge: Yes

LOS ANGELES
Survivors After Suicide
Suicide Prevention Center, Divi-
sion Family Services
Chris Aguiler
626 S. Kingsley Ave.
Los Angeles, CA 90005-2318
(213) 381-5111
(213) 385-3752
Leadership: P/P
Charge: Yes

NAPA
Crisis Help of the North Bay
Toni Ahlgren
P.O. Box 6181
Napa, CA 94581
(707) 252-5560
Leadership: Peer
Charge: No

PACIFIC GROVE
L.O.S.S.
Suicide Prevention & Crisis
Center
Pat Garrigues
P.O. Box 52078
Pacific Grove, CA 93950-7078
(408) 375-6966
Leadership: Peer
Charge: No

REDDING
Help, Inc.
P.O. Box 992498
Redding, CA 96099-2498
(916) 225-5252
Leadership: P/P
Charge: No

REDLANDS
Survivors of Suicide Support
    Group
Susan Joy Neese
923 E. Gail Ave.
Redlands, CA 92374
(714) 792-4862
(714) 387-7668
Leadership: Peer
Charge: No

SACRAMENTO
Friends for Survival, Inc.
Marilyn Koenig
5701 Lerner Way
Sacramento, CA 95823
(916) 392-0664
(916) 967-0742
Leadership: Peer
Charge: No

SAN DIEGO
Sharing & Healing
Al & Linda Vigil
3586 Trenton Ave.
San Diego, CA 92117
(619) 272-3760
(619) 272-1759
Leadership: Peer
Charge: No

SAN DIEGO
Survivors of Suicide (S.O.S.)—
    San Diego
P.O. Box 191176
San Diego, CA 92159
(619) 482-0297, Hotline
    24 hours
Leadership: Peer
Charge: No

SAN FRANCISCO
Self-Help Grief Group
Center for Elderly Suicide Pre-
    vention and Grief
Patrick Arbore
Related Services
4110 Geary Blvd.
San Francisco, CA 94118
(415) 752-2437
Leadership: P/P
Charge: No

SAN JOSE
Survivors of Suicide
Santa Clara Suicide & Crisis
    Service
Crisis Line Volunteers
2220 Moorpark Ave.
San Jose, CA 95128
(408) 279-3312
Leadership: P/P
Charge: Yes

SAN LUIS OBISPO
Suicide Survivor's Group
Hospice of San Luis Obispo
    County, Inc.
P.O. Box 1342
San Luis Obispo, CA 93406

(805) 541-3080
Leadership: P/P
Charge: No

SAN RAFAEL
Grief Counseling Program
Suicide Prevention & Commu-
nity Counseling Service of
Marin
Joan Sheldon
10 N. San Pedro Rd.
San Rafael, CA 94903
(415) 499-1195
Leadership: Prof
Charge: No

SANTA BARBARA
Suicide Survivors
Hospice Services of Santa
Barbara
Michael Pugh, MFCC
222 E. Canon Perdito
Santa Barbara, CA 93101
(805) 965-5555
Leadership: P/P
Charge: No

VACAVILLE
Survivors of Suicide
Charles A. Brown
607 Elmira Rd.
Vacaville, CA 95687
(707) 452-8520
Leadership: Peer
Charge: No

WALNUT CREEK
Survivors of Suicide

Crisis & Suicide Intervention of
Contra Costa
Susan Moore
P.O. Box 4852
Walnut Creek, CA 94596
(415) 944-0645
Leadership: Prof
Charge: No

Colorado

BOULDER
Heartbeat
Dr. Cheryl Clement
710 33d St.
Boulder, CO 80303
(303) 444-3496
Leadership: P/P
Charge: No

COLORADO SPRINGS
Heartbeat
La Rita Archibald
2015 Devon
Colorado Springs, CO 80909
(719) 596-2575
Leadership: Peer
Charge: No

DENVER
Heartbeat
Narice Wheat
1780 S. Bellaire, Ste. 132
Denver, CO 80222
(303) 934-8464
Leadership: Peer
Charge: No

DENVER
Parents of Teen/Young Adult
   Suicides
Vivian Epstein
212 S. Dexter St.
Denver, CO 80222
(303) 322-7450
Leadership: Peer
Charge: No

DENVER
S.O.S.—For Friends & Families
Ivor Richards
Capitol Hill Community Center
Denver, CO 80218
(303) 756-4945
(303) 861-4262
Leadership: P/P
Charge: No

GREELEY
Heartbeat
Weld County Suicide Prevention
   Coalition
Kathy Shannon
1517 16th Ave. Ct.
Greeley, CO 80631
(303) 356-0639
Leadership: P/P
Charge: No

PARKER
Survivors Group
KM Counseling
Karen Dunn
P.O. Box 501
Parker, CO 80134
(303) 841-0259

Leadership: Prof
Charge: Yes

PUEBLO
Heartbeat
Pueblo Suicide Prevention Cen-
   ter, Inc.
Eleanor Hamm
1925 E. Orman, Ste. A-630
Pueblo, CO 81004
(719) 545-2477
(719) 544-1133
Leadership: P/P
Charge: No

Connecticut

DANIELSON
Healing After Suicide
Quinebaug Valley Pastoral
   Counseling Center
Gene McCarthy
P.O. Box 686
Danielson, CT 06239
(203) 774-2145
Leadership: P/P
Charge: No

MIDDLETOWN
Survivors of Suicide
Prof. Clayton Hewitt
Middlesex Community College
100 Training Hill Rd.
Middletown, CT 06457
(203) 344-3043
(203) 347-4003
Leadership: Prof
Charge: No

183

PLAINVILLE
Wheeler Clinic, Inc., Emergency
    Service
Alan Kennedy
91 Northwest Dr.
Plainville, CT 06062
(203) 747-3434
(203) 747-8719
Leadership: Prof
Charge: Yes

STORRS
First Baptist Church
Rev. Bill Keane
P.O. Box 541
Storrs, CT 06268
(203) 429-6043
(203) 429-0673
Leadership: Peer
Charge: No

WEST HARTFORD
Safe Place
The Samaritans
14 Regency Dr.
West Hartford, CT 06110
(203) 232-2121
(203) 232-9559
Leadership: Peer
Charge: No

WETHERSFIELD
Suicide Bereavement
Center for Inner Growth &
    Wholeness, Inc.
JoAnn Mecca
P.O. Box 9185
Wethersfield, CT 06109
(203) 563-3035

Leadership: Peer
Charge: No

Delaware

BETHANY BEACH
Suicide Bereavement
SEASONS Eastern Shore
    Chapter
Cecilia Chodnicki
2 Kent Condo
Jefferson Bridge Rd.
Bethany Beach, DE 19930
(302) 537-9520
(410) 643-6220 Church No.
Leadership: Peer
Charge: No

WILMINGTON
S.O.S.
Ms. Lee Anderson
1813 N. Franklin St.
Wilmington, DE 19802
(302) 652-4485
(302) 656-8308
Leadership: Prof
Charge: No

District of Columbia

WASHINGTON
Andromeda Transcultural Men-
    tal Health Center
1400 Decatur St. NW
Washington, DC 20011
(202) 291-4707
(202) 722-1245
Leadership: P/P
Charge: No

Florida

BRADENTON
Living Afterwards
Anita & Kurt Hosier
3802 33d Ave. Dr. W.
Bradenton, FL 34205
(813) 753-1247
Leadership: P/P
Charge: No

CAPE CORAL
S.O.S. Group
Caring & Coping
1418 S.E. 47th St.
Cape Coral, FL 33904
(813) 945-0338
Leadership: P/P
Charge: No

DAYTONA BEACH
Assure
Mental Health Association of
  Volusia County
Rita Repp
412 S. Palmetto Ave.
P.O. Box 2554
Daytona Beach, FL 32115-2554
(904) 252-5785
(904) 756-3198
Leadership: P/P
Charge: No

FT. LAUDERDALE
Survivors of Suicide
First Call for Help/Broward
  County
Arthur J. Ellick
P.O. Box 14428

Ft. Lauderdale, FL 33302
(305) 467-6333
(305) 524-8371
Leadership: Prof
Charge: No

JACKSONVILLE
Self Help Support Group
Suicide Prevention Center
Sue Boyd
325 E. Duval St.
Jacksonville, FL 32202-2759
(904) 353-2723
Leadership: P/P
Charge: No

MIAMI
Parents of Suicide
Shirley Jaffe
4941 S.W. 71 Pl.
Miami, FL 33155
(305) 666-4756
(305) 271-9000
Leadership: Peer
Charge: No

NAPLES
Survivors of Suicide
Hotline & Referral/Project Help,
  Inc.
Beth Knake
2900 14th St. N., #40
Naples, FL 33940
(813) 649-1404
(800) 329-7227
Leadership: P/P
Charge: No

ORLANDO
Survivors of Suicide

We Care Crisis Center, Inc.
Marge Lindner
112 Pasadena Pl.
Orlando, FL 32803
(407) 425-2624
(407) 628-1227
Leadership: P/P
Charge: No

PENSACOLA
Survivors of Suicide
Mental Health Association/
  Escambia
Karen M. Barber, CEO
1995 N. H St.
Pensacola, FL 32501
(904) 438-9879
Leadership: Prof
Charge: No

PINELLAS PARK
Pinellas Emergency MHS, Inc.
11254 58th St. N.
Pinellas Park, FL 34666-2606
(813) 545-5636
(813) 791-3131
Leadership: Prof
Charge: No

ROCKLEDGE
Crisis Services of Brevard Inc.
P.O. Box 56-1108
Rockledge, FL 32956-1108
(407) 631-8944
Leadership: Prof
Charge: No

TAMPA
Connections

Judith Galle, M.A.
13302-B Winding Oak Ct.
Tampa, FL 33612-3416
(813) 932-1722
Leadership: Prof
Charge: No

Georgia

ALBANY
Suicide Survivors
Prima Kennedy
2823 Dunaway Dr.
Albany, GA 31707-8738
(912) 436-2421
(912) 883-1281
Leadership: P/P
Charge: No

ATLANTA
S.O.S Day Group
Brookwood Center for
  Psychotherapy
Karen Faulk
1708 Peachtree St. NW, Ste. 315
Atlanta, GA 30309
(404) 872-8065
Leadership: P/P
Charge: No

ATLANTA
S.O.S. Sandy Springs Chapter
The Link Counseling Center
Facilitator
348 Mt. Vernon Hwy. NE
Atlanta, GA 30328
(404) 256-9797
Leadership: P/P
Charge: No

LAWRENCEVILLE
S.O.S. Lawrenceville Chapter
Linda Jones
Rock Springs Methodist Church
1100 Rock Springs Rd.
Lawrenceville, GA 30243
(404) 945-4379
Leadership: P/P
Charge: No

MARIETTA
S.O.S. Marietta Chapter
Terri Stamey
56 Whitlock Ave., Rm. 212
Marietta, GA 30060
(404) 432-1621
(404) 436-4090
Leadership: P/P
Charge: No

RIVERDALE
S.O.S. Riverdale Chapter
Morri Lowe
East Side Baptist Church
170 Upper Riverdale Rd.
Riverdale, GA 30274
(404) 478-9243
Leadership: P/P
Charge: No

TUCKER
S.O.S. Tucker Chapter
The Hub
Tom McIntyre, Ph.D.
5165 La Vista Rd.
Tucker, GA 30084
(404) 934-5600
Leadership: P/P
Charge: No

Hawaii

HONOLULU
Survivors of Suicide
Volunteer Information & Refer-
ral Service
Paige Demecilio
680 Iwilei Rd., # 430
Honolulu, HI 96817
(808) 521-4555 24-hr. Crisis Ctr.
Leadership: Prof
Charge: No

Idaho

BOISE
Survivors of Suicide
Richard Jackson
4917 W. Catalpa
Boise, ID 83703
(208) 338-1017
(208) 345-2350
Leadership: Peer
Charge: No

IDAHO FALLS
Survivors of Suicide, Inc.
Elaine Sullivan
2411 S. Woodruff
Idaho Falls, ID 83404
(208) 524-2411
Leadership: Peer
Charge: No

Illinois

AURORA
Survivors of Suicide
S. Weber-Slepicka
206 S. Fordham

Aurora, IL 60506
(708) 897-5531
(708) 897-9699
Leadership: P/P
Charge: No

CHICAGO
Loving Outreach to Survivors of
  Suicide
Rev. Charles Rubey
Catholic Charities
126 N. DesPlaines St.
Chicago, IL 60661-2357
(312) 876-2260
Leadership: P/P
Charge: No

CHICAGO
OPTIONS Counseling Service
Janet Migdow
3232 W. Victoria
Chicago, IL 60659
(312) 463-1901
Leadership: Prof
Charge: Yes

EDGEMONT
Survivors of Suicide
Call for Help, Suicide & Crisis
  Intervention
Marcie Ehret
9400 Lebanon Rd.
Edgemont, IL 62203
(618) 397-0963
Leadership: P/P
Charge: No

MATTOON
Survivors of Suicide

Hospice of Lincolnland
Don Murphy
75 Professional Plaza
Mattoon, IL 61938
(217) 234-4044
Leadership: Prof
Charge: No

OAK BROOK
The Compassionate Friends,
  Inc.
S. Salisbury-Richard
P.O. Box 3696
Oak Brook, IL 60522-3696
(708) 990-0010
Leadership: Peer
Charge: No

PEORIA
Survivors of Suicide
Mental Health Association of
  Illinois Valley
Rev. Eimo Hinrichs
5407 N. University
Peoria, IL 61614
(309) 693-5281
(309) 697-3342
Leadership: P/P
Charge: No

Indiana

BLOOMINGTON
S.O.S./Heartbeat
Rev. John Vanderzee
P.O. Box 1149
Bloomington, IN 47402
(812) 336-9463
Leadership: P/P
Charge: No

COLUMBUS
Heartbeat/S.O.S.
Nancy Owens
16210 E. Main St.
Columbus, IN 47203
(812) 546-5820
Leadership: Peer
Charge: No

EVANSVILLE
Survivors of Suicide
MH Association in Vanderburgh
   County
Dr. Helen Smith
1018 Lincoln Ave.
Evansville, IN 47715
(812) 426-2640
Leadership: P/P
Charge: No

FORT WAYNE
We the Living
Viola Sedlacek
9347 Marydale La.
Fort Wayne, IN 46804
(219) 422-6402
(219) 432-6293
Leadership: Peer
Charge: No

HAMMOND
Stress
MHA in Lake County
2450 169th St.
Hammond, IN 46323
(219) 845-2720
Leadership: Peer
Charge: No

INDIANAPOLIS
Survivors of Suicide Victims
Chaplains' Office
Jim Gaynor
Community Hospital of
   Indianapolis
Indianapolis, IN 46219
(317) 355-4743
Leadership: P/P
Charge: No

Iowa

CEDAR RAPIDS
Suicide Survivors Group
Foundation II, Inc.
Karen O'Brien
1540 2d Ave. SE
Cedar Rapids, IA 52403
(319) 362-2174
(800) 332-4224
Leadership: P/P
Charge: No

IOWA CITY
Ray of Hope, Inc.
E. Betsy Ross
P.O. Box 2323
Iowa City, IA 52244
(319) 337-9890
Leadership: P/P
Charge: No

IOWA CITY
Suicide Survivors Support
   Group Crisis Center
Vince Matulionis
321 E. 1st St.
Iowa City, IA 52240

(319) 351-0140
Leadership: P/P
Charge: No

Kansas

PARSONS
Suicide Prevention Program
Parsons Ray of Hope
Ann Gorrell
704 Creek
Parsons, KS 67357
(316) 421-3254
Leadership: P/P
Charge: No

TOPEKA
Survivors of Suicide
Bonnie Brickhouse
3019 S.E. Starlite
Topeka, KS 66605
(913) 267-4547
(913) 233-1730
Leadership: P/P
Charge: No

Kentucky

LEXINGTON
Survivors of Suicide
Bluegrass Chapter
Carolyn Elliott
1450 Newton Pl.
Lexington, KY 40511
(606) 253-1331
Leadership: P/P
Charge: No

LOUISVILLE
Survivors of Suicide Inc.

Jonnie Hoge
East/Southwest
330 N. Hubbard's La.
Louisville, KY 40207
(502) 895-9122
(502) 589-4313
Leadership: Prof
Charge: No

MIDDLESBORO
Survivors of Suicide
Lonnie Brooks
P.O. Box Z
Middlesboro, KY 40965
(606) 248-1678
(606) 248-7616
Leadership: Peer
Charge: No

Louisiana

BATON ROUGE
Baton Rouge Crisis Intervention
   Center, Inc.
Frank R. Campbell
4837 Revere Ave.
Baton Rouge, LA 70808
(504) 924-1431
(504) 924-3900
Leadership: P/P
Charge: No

MONROE
Support After Suicide
Jim & Barbara Moore
3804 Gouville Dr.
Monroe, LA 71201
(318) 323-9479
(318) 322-5065

Leadership: Peer
Charge: No

NEW ORLEANS
Coping With Suicide
Roma Monlezun
2506 State St.
New Orleans, LA 70118
(504) 866-3792
Leadership: Peer
Charge: No

Maine

BANGOR
Safe Place
Barbara C. Smith
All Souls Church
State St.
Bangor, ME 04401
(207) 947-7003
(207) 942-8815
Leadership: P/P
Charge: No

LEWISTON
Suicide Survivors Support
  Group
Irene Bernier
Lewiston, ME
(207) 786-2867
Leadership: Peer
Charge: No

PORTLAND
Suicide Survivors Group
Maine Medical Center
Connie Korda
22 Bramhall St.

Portland, ME 04102
(207) 781-4226
(207) 781-4775
Leadership: Prof
Charge: No

Maryland

ARNOLD
Growing Through Grief, Inc.
Betty Bartow
P.O. Box 269
Arnold, MD 21012
(410) 974-4769 Bill Griswold
(410) 721-0899
Leadership: Prof
Charge: No

BALTIMORE
SEASONS: Suicide Bereavement
Dorothy Schanberger
4706 Meise Dr.
Baltimore, MD 21206
(410) 882-2937 Jack
  Schanberger
Leadership: Peer
Charge: No

BETHESDA
SEASONS: Suicide Bereavement
Glenis Bellais
Cedar Lane Uniterian Church
9601 Cedar La.
Bethesda, MD 20814
(301) 493-8302
Leadership: Peer
Charge: No

LANHAM
Prince George's County Hotline
& Suicide Prevention Center
Rhonda Gibson
9300 Annapolis Rd., #100
Lanham, MD 20706
(301) 731-4922
Leadership: P/P
Charge: No

ROCKVILLE
SEASONS: Suicide Bereavement
Coryne Melton
13907 Vista Dr.
Rockville, MD 20853
(301) 460-4677
Leadership: Peer
Charge: No

WESTMINSTER
Suicide Bereavement
SEASONS
Ann Hepding
1911 Patricia Ct.
Westminster, MD 21157
(301) 876-1047
Leadership: Peer
Charge: No

Massachusetts

CAMBRIDGE
After Suicide
Focus Counseling & Consulting
Inc.
Mimi Elmer, LICSW
186-1/2 Hampshire St.
Cambridge, MA 02139
(617) 876-4488 Mimi Elmer,
LICSW

(617) 738-7668 Dorothy
Koerner, LICSW
Leadership: Prof
Charge: Yes

CONCORD
Survivors of Suicide
Geoffry B. Smith
290 Baker Ave., Ste. N227
Concord, MA 01742
(508) 369-4205
Leadership: Prof
Charge: Yes

FALL RIVER
Safe Place Self-Help Support
Group
Samaritans of Fall River/New
Bedford
Ellie Leite
386 Stanley St.
Fall River, MA 02720
(508) 673-3777
(508) 999-7267
Leadership: Peer
Charge: No

FRAMINGHAM
Safe Place/Samaritans
Samaritans of South Middlesex
Jim Hunt
73 Union Ave.
Framingham, MA 01701
(508) 875-4500
(508) 478-7877
Leadership: Peer
Charge: No

HYANNIS
In Memory Still

Catholic Social Services
Bob Fournier
261 South St.
Hyannis, MA 02601
(508) 771-6771
Leadership: P/P
Charge: No

METHUEN
Safe Place/Samaritans
Samaritans of Merrimack Valley
Margaret Serley
169 East St.
Methuen, MA 01844
(508) 688-6607
Leadership: Peer
Charge: No

PITTSFIELD
Suicide Loss Support Group
HospiceCare in the Berkshires
Julie McCarthy
P.O. Box 2036
235 East St.
Pittsfield, MA 01202
(413) 443-2994
Leadership: P/P
Charge: Yes

Michigan

ANN ARBOR
Survivors of Suicide
University of Michigan Hospital
Marlene M. Giroux
UH9C-9150, Box 0120
1500 E. Medical Center Dr.
Ann Arbor, MI 48109
(313) 936-6462

Leadership: Prof
Charge: Yes

BAY CITY
Dorothy Navidzadeh Chapter
S.O.S. Support Group
Mary Ann Carrier
3451 Euclid Ct.
Bay City, MI 48706
(517) 684-5514
(517) 684-9393
Leadership: P/P
Charge: No

BAY CITY
S.O.S. Group—St. Vincent de
    Paul
Mary Anne Carrier
St. Vincent de Paul
Bay City, MI 48706
(517) 684-5514
Leadership: P/P
Charge: No

BIRMINGHAM
Those Touched by Suicide
Facilitator
1775 Melton
Birmingham, MI 48009
(313) 646-5224
Leadership: Peer
Charge: No

CADILLAC
Survivors of Suicide
North Central Community MH
Melissa Sjogran
527 Cobbs
Cadillac, MI 49601

(616) 775-3463
(616) 826-3865
Jackie Adams
Leadership: Peer
Charge: No

DETROIT
Survivors of Suicide
NSO Emergency Telephone
    Serv/SP Center
Mary Leonhardi
220 Bagley, Ste. 626
Detroit, MI 48226
(313) 224-7000
Leadership: P/P
Charge: No

EDWARDSBURG
Michiana S.O.S. Support Group
Cheryl Allen-Hicks
23851 May St.
Edwardsburg, MI 49112
(616) 699-7472
Leadership: Peer
Charge: No

FLINT
Catholic Social Services
Alice Sager
202 E. Boulevard Dr., Ste. 210
Flint, MI 48503
(313) 232-9950
Leadership: P/P
Charge: No

GRAND RAPIDS
West Michigan Survivors of
    Suicide
Ethel Bucek

1777 Pineknoll SE
Grand Rapids, MI 49508
(616) 455-0372
(616) 865-3555
Leadership: Peer
Charge: No

KALAMAZOO
Gryphon Place
Jack Klott
1104 S. Westnedge
Kalamazoo, MI 49008
(616) 381-1510
Leadership: Prof
Charge: No

PORT HURON
St. Clair County Community
    Mental Health Services
Mary Ludtke
1011 Military St.
Port Huron, MI 48060
(313) 985-8900
Leadership: P/P
Charge: No

SAGINAW
S.O.S. Group
Saginaw General Hospital
Barb Smith
7165 Burmeister
Saginaw, MI 48609
(517) 781-0410
(517) 791-4410 Kathy Hartwick
Leadership: P/P
Charge: No

Minnesota

DULUTH
Suicide Survivors Support
  Group
St. Mary's Grief Support Center
Ben Wolfe
407 E. 3d St.
Duluth, MN 55805
(218) 726-4402
Leadership: Peer
Charge: No

GOLDEN VALLEY
Suicide Survivors Grief Group
Sara Jaehne
1792 Maryland Ave. N.
Golden Valley, MN 55427
(612) 544-9651
Leadership: Peer
Charge: No

MANKATO
Suicide Grief Support Group
Kenneth J. Good
Mankato State University,
  Psychology
MSU Box 35, P.O. Box 8400
Mankato, MN 56002-8400
(507) 931-6471
(507) 257-3372
Leadership: Peer
Charge: No

MINNEAPOLIS
Death Response Team
University of Minnesota
Ralph Rickgarn

Comstock Hall East—Housing
  Services
210 Delaware St. SE
Minneapolis, MN 55455-0307
(612) 624-2994
Leadership: Prof
Charge: No

MINNEAPOLIS
Suicide Survivors Grief Group-
  Burnsville
Afterwords Publishing Group
Adina Wrobleski
2615 Park Ave., Ste. 506
Minneapolis, MN 55407
(612) 871-0068
Leadership: Peer
Charge: No

MINNEAPOLIS
Suicide Grief Support Group
Grace U. Lutheran Church
Anyone at Location
Harvard & Delaware Sts. SE
Minneapolis, MN 55414
(612) 379-1363
(612) 331-8125
Leadership: Peer
Charge: No

ST. PAUL
Survivors of Suicide
Tony Del Percio
1485 White Bear Ave.
St. Paul, MN 55106
(612) 776-1565
Leadership: Prof
Charge: No

Mississippi

STARKVILLE
Survivors of Suicide
Karen C. Lewis
1200 Nottingham Rd.
Starkville, MS 39759
(601) 324-9215
Leadership: Peer
Charge: No

Missouri

JOPLIN
Joplin Ray of Hope
SuAn Richardson
Missouri Southern State College
3950 Newman Rd.
Joplin, MO 64801-1595
(417) 625-9300
(417) 358-1373
Leadership: Peer
Charge: No

ST. LOUIS
Survivors of Suicide Support
    Group
Life Crisis Services, Inc.
Nancy Collins
1423 S. Big Bend Blvd.
St. Louis, MO 63117
(314) 647-3100
(314) 647-4357 24-hr. hotline
Leadership: P/P
Charge: No

Nebraska

HASTINGS
Heartbeat

Barbara Marsh
1740 Highland Dr.
Hastings, NE 68901
(402) 463-7804
Leadership: P/P
Charge: No

LINCOLN
Lincoln Ray of Hope
Delmary Wiltshire
2118 S. 36th St.
Lincoln, NE 68506
(402) 488-3827
(402) 447-8610 Gary & Jenifer
    Nelson
Leadership: P/P
Charge: No

NORFOLK
Norfolk Ray of Hope
Charlotte Teuscher
1507 Glenmore, Apt. 303
Norfolk, NE 68701
(402) 379-2460
(402) 379-0712
Leadership: P/P
Charge: No

OMAHA
Omaha Ray of Hope
Michael Miller, Ph.D.
Metropolitan Technical Commu-
    nity College
P.O. Box 3777
Omaha, NE 68103
(402) 289-1205
Leadership: P/P
Charge: No

Nevada

RENO
Suicide Prevention & Crisis Call
  Center
Facilitator
P.O. Box 8016
Reno, NV 89507
(702) 323-6111
(800) 992-5757
Leadership: P/P
Charge: No

New Hampshire

BEDFORD
Bedford Counseling Associates
Toni Paul
25 S. River Rd.
Bedford Square
Bedford, NH 03102
(603) 623-1916
Leadership: Prof
Charge: Yes

CONCORD
Central NH Community MH Ser-
  vices Inc.
Nancy J. Churchill
5 Market La.
P.O. Box 2032
Concord, NH 03301
(603) 228-1551
Leadership: P/P
Charge: Yes

KEENE
Samaritans/Safe Place
The Samaritans of Keene

Facilitator
69-Z Island St.
Keene, NH 03431
(603) 357-5505
Leadership: Prof
Charge: No

MANCHESTER
Mental Health Center of Greater
  Manchester
T. Paul, C. J. Warren
401 Cypress St.
Manchester, NH 03103
(603) 668-4111
Leadership: Prof
Charge: Yes

MANCHESTER
S.O.S. Survivors of Suicide
Samaritans of South Central NH
Susan Pendleton
2013 Elm St.
Manchester, NH 03104
(603) 644-2525
Leadership: Peer
Charge: No

SALEM
Coping with a Loved One's
  Suicide
Center for Life Management
Amy Metcalf, MSN, CS
Salem Professional Park
44 Stiles Rd.
Salem, NH 03079
(603) 893-3548
(603) 432-1500, Ext. 133
Leadership: Prof
Charge: No

197

New Jersey

ANDOVER
Survivors of Suicide
Jane L. Cole
P.O. Box 183
Andover, NJ 07821
(201) 786-5178
Leadership: Peer
Charge: No

DUMONT
Survivors After Suicide CCMH
Rachel Gur-Arie
2 Park Ave.
Dumont, NJ 07628
(201) 385-4400
Leadership: P/P
Charge: No

PISCATAWAY
Survivors of Suicide
UMDNJ Community Mental
    Health at Piscataway
Karen Dunne-Maxim
671 Hoes La.
Piscataway, NJ 08854
(908) 463-4136
Leadership: P/P
Charge: No

TOMS RIVER
Survivors of Suicide
Community Medical Center
Peter Silva
The Center for Kids & Family
Riverwood II Building
Toms River, NJ 08753
(908) 505-5437

Leadership: P/P
Charge: No

WOODBURY
Survivors of Suicide
Community MH Center for
    Gloucester County
Sonia J. Klimoff
404 Tatum St.
Woodbury, NJ 08096
(609) 845-8050
Leadership: P/P
Charge: No

New Mexico

ALBUQUERQUE
New Mexico Grief Intervention
    Program
Carol Chapin
Office Of Medical
    Investigator
UNM School of Medicine
Albuquerque, NM 87131
(505) 277-3053
Leadership: Prof
Charge: No

New York

ALBANY
Safe Place/Samaritans
Eileen Reardon
200 Central Ave.
Albany, NY 12206
(518) 463-0861
(518) 463-2323
Leadership: Peer
Charge: No

BALLSTON SPA
Safe Place/Samaritans
Eileen Reardon
202 Milton Ave.
Ballston Spa, NY 12020
(518) 463-0861
Leadership: Peer
Charge: No

BROOKLYN
Friends And Relatives
Christine Giangreco
27 Schermerhorn St.
Brooklyn, NY 11201
(718) 643-1946
Leadership: Peer
Charge: No

BUFFALO
Life Transitions Center, Inc.
Marian Ciaranella
3580 Harlem Rd.
Buffalo, NY 14215
(716) 836-6460
Leadership: Peer
Charge: Yes

BUFFALO
Suicide Bereavement Group
Thomas Frantz, Ph.D.
Life Transition Center
3580 Harlem Rd.
Buffalo, NY 14215
(716) 636-3152, Thomas Frantz,
   Ph.D.
(716) 636-3152, Ralph Klicker
Leadership: Peer
Charge: No

CORTLAND
Survivors of Suicide Support
Mardis Kelsen
c/o Judge Kelsen
15 Terrace Rd.
Cortland, NY 13045
(607) 756-2352
(607) 836-6345
Leadership: Peer
Charge: No

FISHKILL
St. Francis Bereavement Center
Sr. Jean Canora
Blodgett Library
Bedford Ave.
Fishkill, NY 12524
(914) 452-1400, Ext. 4214
Leadership: Peer
Charge: No

FLORAL PARK
Transitions
Roslyn Marcus, ACSW
174 Jericho Tnpk.
Floral Park, NY 11001
(516) 488-7697
Leadership: Prof
Charge: Yes

FLUSHING
Survivors of Suicide
St. Andrew Avellino Rectory
Sr. Mary Stephen
35-60 158th St.
Flushing, NY 11358
(718) 359-5276
(718) 359-0417

Leadership: P/P
Charge: No

GOSHEN
Survivors of Suicide Support
  Group
Wanda Hall
Orange County Department Of
  Mental Health
Harriman Dr.
Goshen, NY 10924
(914) 294-6185
Leadership: Prof
Charge: No

HEMPSTEAD L.I.
Family Services Association of
  Nassau County Inc.
Mike Miller
The Bereavement Center
129 Jackson St.
Hempstead L.I., NY 11550
(516) 485-4600
Leadership: Prof
Charge: Yes

HYDE PARK
Bereavement Support Group
Hyde Park Memorial
Sr. Jean Canora
Albany Post Rd.
(next to Darrow's Funeral
  Home)
Hyde Park, NY 12538
(914) 452-1400, Ext. 4214
Leadership: Peer
Charge: No

ITHACA
Postvention Coordinator

Suicide Prevention & Crisis Ser-
  vice of Tompkins County
P.O. Box 312
Ithaca, NY 14851
(607) 272-1505
Leadership: Prof
Charge: No

NEW YORK
The Samaritans of New York
  City
Alan Ross
P.O. Box 1259
Madison Square Sta.
New York, NY 10159
(212) 673-3000
Leadership: Peer
Charge: No

NEW YORK
Survivors of Suicide
Regent Hospital
Iona Able
425 E. 61st St.
New York, NY 10021
(212) 935-3400
Leadership: P/P
Charge: No

PERU
Harvest
Colleen Bonnier
Rd. 1, Box 173H
Peru, NY 12972
(518) 643-8199
Leadership: P/P
Charge: No

PLAINVIEW
Survivors of Suicide Group

Phylis Chase
1117 Old Country Rd.
Plainview, NY 11803
(516) 938-7233
(516) 365-5810
Leadership: Prof
Charge: Yes

ROCHESTER
After Suicide
Betty Becker
34 Alford St.
Rochester, NY 14609
(716) 654-7262
(716) 265-0449
Leadership: Peer
Charge: No

ROSLYN HEIGHTS
North Shore Child & Family
  Guidance Center
Edward Paley
480 Old Westbury Rd.
Roslyn Heights, NY 11577
(516) 626-1971
Leadership: P/P
Charge: No

SCHENECTADY
Schenectady Support Group for
  Suicide
Marianne Venneman
94 Western Pkwy.
Schenectady, NY 12304
(518) 372-1900
Leadership: Prof
Charge: No

STATEN ISLAND
Survivors of Suicide

Jean Jamate
350 Richmond Terr., Apt. 6N
Staten Island, NY 10301
(718) 448-3306
Leadership: Peer
Charge: No

YORKTOWN HEIGHTS
Surviving Suicide
Ann Smolin
2000 Maple Hill St.
Yorktown Heights, NY 10595
(914) 962-5593
Leadership: Prof
Charge: No

North Carolina

CHARLOTTE
Touched By Suicide
To Life
Howard Winokuer
P.O. Box 9354
Charlotte, NC 28299
(704) 332-5433
Leadership: Prof
Charge: Yes

MOUNT AIRY
Survivors of Suicide
Myra Reddie
Hospice of Surry County, Inc.
P.O. Box 1034
Mount Airy, NC 27030
(919) 789-2922
Leadership: Prof
Charge: No

WILMINGTON
Touched by Suicide/Wilmington

Adrian Shepard
801 Pine Forest Rd.
Wilmington, NC 28409
(919) 392-6818
(919) 791-6383
Leadership: Peer
Charge: No

North Dakota

BISMARCK
Survivors of Suicide
Corky Titus
200 W. Bowen
Bismarck, ND 58504
(701) 255-3692
(701) 255-3090
Leadership: P/P
Charge: No

BISMARCK
Grief After Suicide
MH Association of North Dakota
Loretta Bierdeman
200 W. Bowen Ave.
Bismarck, ND 58504
(701) 255-3692
(701) 255-3090
Leadership: P/P
Charge: No

GRAND FORKS
Friends and Family Surviving
    Suicide
Northeast Human Service Cen-
    ter
Cynthia B. Schaefer
1407 24th Ave. S.
Grand Forks, ND 58201

(701) 746-9411
Leadership: P/P
Charge: No

Ohio

AKRON
Survivors
Portage Path Community Mental
    Health Center
Andrea Denton
150 Cross St.
Akron, OH 44311
(216) 253-9388
Leadership: Prof
Charge: No

CANTON
Survivors
Crisis Intervention Center of
    Stark County
Kimberly M. Leggett
2421 13th St., NW
Canton, OH 44708
(216) 452-6000
Leadership: Prof
Charge: No

COLUMBUS
Survivors of Suicide
Carol Stewart
192 S. Princeton Ave.
Columbus, OH 43223
(614) 279-9382
Leadership: Peer
Charge: No

DAYTON
Survivors of Suicide

Suicide Prevention Center, Inc.
P.O. Box 1393
Dayton, OH 45401-1393
(513) 297-4777
(513) 297-9096
Leadership: P/P
Charge: No

DELAWARE
Help Anonymous, Inc.
Lesia Krisa
11 E. Central Ave.
Delaware, OH 43015
(614) 369-3316
(614) 548-7324
Leadership: P/P
Charge: No

MT. GILEAD
Hope Line, Inc.
Cherry Bennett
950 Meadow Dr.
Mt. Gilead, OH 43338
(419) 947-2520
Leadership: P/P
Charge: No

SPRINGFIELD
Survivors of Suicide
Mental Health Services—Clark
   County
Elizabeth Martin
1345 Fountain Blvd.
Springfield, OH 45504
(513) 399-9500
Leadership: P/P
Charge: No

URBANA
Survivors of Suicide

B McDaniel Oetting
Tanglewood Acres
4621 Storms Creek Rd.
Urbana, OH 43078
(513) 788-2575
Leadership: P/P
Charge: No

WESTERVILLE
S.O.S.
Concord Counseling Center
Barb Smith
924 Eastwind Dr.
Westerville, OH 43081
(614) 882-9338
Leadership: Prof
Charge: No

YOUNGSTOWN
Survivors of Suicide
Help Hotline Crisis Center, Inc.
Cathy Grizinski
P.O. Box 46
Youngstown, OH 44501
(216) 747-5111
(216) 747-2696
Leadership: P/P
Charge: No

Oklahoma

OKLAHOMA CITY
S.O.S.
Oklahoma City Chapter
William H. "Bill" Pulley
4304 N.W. 16th Terr.
Oklahoma City, OK 73107
(405) 942-1345
Leadership: Peer
Charge: No

TULSA
Survivors
Mental Health Association
Direct Services Coordinator
1870 S. Boulder
Tulsa, OK 74119
(918) 585-1213
Leadership: P/P
Charge: No

Ontario

LONDON
Survivors of Suicide
Canadian Mental Health Association
Bonnie A. Williams
355 Princess Ave.
London, ON N6B 2A7
Canada
(519) 434-9178
Leadership: P/P
Charge: No

TORONTO
Survivor Support Program
Karen Letofsky
10 Trinity Sq.
Toronto, ON M5G 1B1
Canada
(416) 595-1716
Leadership: P/P
Charge: No

WINDSOR
Bereavement Resources
Canadian Mental Health Association

Bereavement Spec.
880 Ouellette Ave., Ste. 901
Windsor, ON N9A 1C7
Canada
(519) 255-7440
Leadership: Peer
Charge: No

Oregon

EUGENE
Survivors of Suicide
Diane Gregoire
5053 Alpine Lp.
Eugene, OR 97405
(503) 343-3269
Leadership: Peer
Charge: Yes

PORTLAND
Hopewell House
John McClure
6171 SW Capital Hwy.
Portland, OR 97201
(503) 244-7890
(503) 226-7620
Leadership: Prof
Charge: Yes

PORTLAND
Suicide Bereavement Support
Virginia Bender
P.O. Box 12471
Portland, OR 97212
(503) 284-7426
(503) 235-0476
Leadership: Peer
Charge: No

PORTLAND
The Dougy Center (ages 6–19)
Donna Schuurman Ed.D.
3909 S.E. 52d
P.O. Box 86852
Portland, OR 97286
(503) 775-5683
Leadership: Peer
Charge: Yes

Pennsylvania

ALTOONA
Altoona Hospital Community
   MH Center
Judy Clouser
620 Howard Ave.
Altoona, PA 16601-4899
(814) 946-2488
Leadership: P/P
Charge: No

BUTLER
Survivors of Suicide
Pamela V. Grabe
124 W. Cunningham St.
Butler, PA 16001
(412) 287-1965
Leadership: P/P
Charge: No

ELKINS PARK
Survivors of Suicide
Dr. Marvin Rubin
c/o the Bereavement Center
8033 Old York Rd. Ste. 100
Elkins Park, PA 19117
(215) 635-4090
(215) 338-9934

Leadership: P/P
Charge: No

FOLCROFT
S.O.S. Inc.
Mary Ellen Carpenter
2064 Heather Rd.
Folcroft, PA 19032
(215) 586-5171
Leadership: Peer
Charge: No

FORT WASHINGTON
Survivors of Suicide, Inc.
Northwestern Institute
450 Bethlehem Pk.
Fort Washington, PA 19034
(215) 745-8247
Leadership: Peer
Charge: No

LANCASTER
Survivors of Suicide Support
   Group
Susan J. DeLong
1120 Hempfield Dr.
Lancaster, PA 17601
(717) 898-8239
Leadership: Peer
Charge: No

LANGHORNE
Survivors of Suicide
Delaware Valley Medical Center
200 Oxford Valley Rd.
Langhorne, PA 19047
(215) 745-8247
Leadership: Peer
Charge: No

LEWISBURG
S.O.S.
Elizabeth Chadwick
Rd. 1, Box 426
Lewisburg, PA 17837
(717) 523-7509
Leadership: P/P
Charge: No

MECHANICSBURG
Suicide Bereavement Group
Beverly Aument
960 Century Dr.
P.O. Box 2001
Mechanicsburg, PA 17055
(717) 795-0330
Leadership: Prof
Charge: Yes

MONACA
Suicide's Other Victims
MH Association Beaver County
Mary Kay Russo
1260 N. Brodhead Rd., Ste. 107
Monaca, PA 15061
(412) 775-4165
(412) 775-8523 FAX
Leadership: P/P
Charge: No

MORRISVILLE
Survivors of Suicide Support
   Group
Betty Coatsworth
37 Walnut La.
Morrisville, PA 19067
(215) 736-1643
Leadership: Peer
Charge: No

PHILADELPHIA
Albert Einstein Medical Center
Bonnie Frank Carter
5501 Old York Rd.
Philadelphia, PA 19141-3098
(215) 456-8072
(215) 456-7240
Leadership: Prof
Charge: Yes

PHILADELPHIA
Phil., Mont., Delaw., & Bucks
   County Survivors of Suicide,
   Inc.
Bernard Kaplan
1113 Kerper St.
Philadelphia, PA 19111
(215) 745-8247
(215) 545-2242
Leadership: Peer
Charge: No

PHILADELPHIA
Survivors of Suicide, Inc.
The Graduate Hospital
18th & Lombard Sts.
Philadelphia, PA 19146
(215) 545-2242
Leadership: Peer
Charge: No

PITTSBURGH
Survivors of Suicide
Western Psychiatric Institute &
   Clinic
Grace M. Moritz
3811 O'Hara St.
Pittsburgh, PA 15213
(412) 624-3674

(412) 624-3786
Leadership: Prof
Charge: No

QUAKERTOWN
Survivors of Suicide
Anne Landis
328 Park Ave.
Quakertown, PA 18951
(215) 536-0910
(215) 536-5143
Leadership: Peer
Charge: No

SCRANTON
Suicide Survivors Group
Gary Vanscoy
Catholic Social Services
400 Wyoming Ave.
Scranton, PA 18503
(717) 346-8936
Leadership: P/P
Charge: No

SHARON
Survivors of Suicide
Bill Shannon
318 W. State St.
Sharon, PA 16146
(412) 342-5410
(412) 347-1303
Leadership: Peer
Charge: No

UPLAND
Survivors of Suicide, Inc.
Crozer-Chester Medical Center
One Medical Center Blvd.
Upland, PA 19013

(215) 586-5171
Leadership: Peer
Charge: No

Quebec

CHICOUTIMI
Saguenay-Lac-St. Jean Centre de
    Prevention du Suicide 02
C.P. 993
Chicoutimi, PQ G7H 5G4
Canada
(418) 545-9110
Leadership: Prof
Charge: No

QUEBEC
Centre de Prevention du Sui-
    cide, CPS.
Linda Delisle
141 rue St. Jean
Quebec, PQ G1R 1N4
Canada
(418) 525-4588
(418) 525-4628, Sophie Pechere
Leadership: Prof
Charge: No

Rhode Island

PROVIDENCE
Safe Place/Samaritans
The Samaritans of Rhode Island
Eunice Bishop
2 Magee St.
Providence, RI 02906
(401) 272-4044
Leadership: Prof
Charge: No

South Carolina

GREENVILLE
Survivors of Suicide
Rowland Hyde
3 McPherson La.
Greenville, SC 29605
(803) 271-8888
(803) 235-6035
Leadership: Peer
Charge: No

LEXINGTON
Survivors of Suicide
Cathy Neeley
601 Queenland Ct.
Lexington, SC 29072
(803) 356-2874
(803) 798-4804
Leadership: P/P
Charge: No

N. CHARLESTON
Survivors of Suicide Hotline
P.O. Box 71583
N. Charleston, SC 29415-1583
(803) 747-3007
(803) 744-4357
Leadership: P/P
Charge: No

South Dakota

SIOUX FALLS
Survivors of Suicide
Candice Cummings
Family Services
300 E. 8th St.
Sioux Falls, SD 57102

(605) 336-1974
Leadership: Prof
Charge: No

Tennessee

NASHVILLE
Survivors of Suicide Support
  Groups
Crisis Intervention Center, Inc.
Kitty Sanders
P.O. Box 40752
Nashville, TN 37204-0752
(615) 244-7444
(615) 255-4357
Leadership: P/P
Charge: No

Texas

AMARILLO
Survivors Group
Suicide & Crisis Center
Vicki Eden
P.O. Box 3250
Amarillo, TX 79116-3250
(806) 359-6699
Leadership: P/P
Charge: No

AUSTIN
Survivors of Suicide
Hotline to Help
Melissa Ward
Austin-Travis County MHMR
P.O. Box 3548
Austin, TX 78764-3548
(512) 440-4085
(512) 472-4357

Leadership: P/P
Charge: No

CORPUS CHRISTI
Survivors After Suicide
Madelyn Olson
4021 Acushnet, Apt. A
Corpus Christi, TX 78413
(512) 853-1964
(512) 993-9700
Leadership: Peer
Charge: No

DALLAS
Suicide and Crisis Center
Debbie Meripolski
2808 Swiss Ave.
Dallas, TX 75204
(214) 828-1000
Leadership: P/P
Charge: No

FT. WORTH
Survivors of Suicide Inc.
Mary I. Archer
P.O. Box 10614
Ft. Worth, TX 76114
(817) 654-5343
(817) 732-6049
Leadership: P/P
Charge: No

HELOTES
Survivors Of Loved One's Suicide
S.O.L.O.S.
Pat O'Brien
10006 Lazy J Trail
Helotes, TX 78023

(512) 695-9136
(512) 616-0885
Leadership: Peer
Charge: No

HOUSTON
Crisis Intervention of Houston,
Inc.
Pat Whitten-Lege
P.O. Box 130866
Houston, TX 77219
(713) 527-9864
(713) 228-1505
Leadership: P/P
Charge: No

LUBBOCK
Survivors of Suicide Support
Group
Contact Lubbock
Sandra Stendahl, MTS
P.O. Box 6477
Lubbock, TX 79493-6477
(806) 765-7272
(806) 765-8393
Leadership: P/P
Charge: No

PLANO
Survivors of Suicide
Crisis Center of Collin County
Nancy DeStefano
P.O. Box 861808
Plano, TX 75086-1808
(214) 881-0088
(214) 542-8500
Leadership: P/P
Charge: No

SAN ANGELO
Survivors Group
MHMR Service for the Concho
    Valley
Holly Hallman
224 N. Magdalen
San Angelo, TX 76903
(915) 655-8965
Leadership: P/P
Charge: No

Utah

LAYTON
Legacy
Judy or Don Bezoski
2684 N. 2700 E.
Layton, UT 84040
(801) 771-8476
(801) 394-5556
Leadership: Peer
Charge: No

PARK CITY
SEASONS
Christina Larsen
P.O. Box 187
Park City, UT 84060
(801) 649-8327
Leadership: Peer
Charge: No

Vermont

BURLINGTON
Persons Left Behind by Suicide
Edwin Granai
106 Killarney Dr.
Burlington, VT 05401
(802) 658-3774

Leadership: Prof
Charge: No

Virginia

FAIRFAX
Suicide Survivor Support Group
Helen Fitzgerald
3601 Devilwood Ct.
Fairfax, VA 22030
(703) 866-2100
(703) 273-3454
Leadership: P/P
Charge: No

NEWPORT NEWS
Survivors of Suicide Group
Tom Crossman
Catholic Charities
12829 Jefferson Ave., Ste. 101
Newport News, VA 23602
(804) 875-0060
(804) 591-2418
Leadership: P/P
Charge: No

PORTSMOUTH
Suicide-Crisis Center, Inc.
P.O. Box 1493
Portsmouth, VA 23705
(804) 627-5433, Tidewater
    Psych.
(804) 483-3404, Churchland
    Psych.
Leadership: Peer
Charge: No

RICHMOND
Surviving Group

Department Of Mental Health
Penny Ginger
501 N. 9th St., #237
Richmond, VA 23219
(804) 780-6911
Leadership: P/P
Charge: No

VIRGINIA BEACH
Survivors of Suicide
Tidewater Psychiatric Institute
LeeAnn Lane-Malbon
1701 Will-O-Wisp Dr.
Virginia Beach, VA 23454
(804) 481-1211
(804) 627-5433
Leadership: Prof
Charge: No

WINCHESTER
Survivors of Suicide Support
   Group
Helen DeMoya
312 Russellcroft Rd.
Winchester, VA 22601
(703) 667-1178
Leadership: Peer
Charge: No

Washington

AUBURN
King County S.O.S. in Auburn
Bible Baptist Church
Lois & Bryon Knowles
1320 Auburn Way S.
Auburn, WA 98002
(206) 833-7127
Leadership: Peer
Charge: No

BOTHELL
Survivors of Suicide
Facilitator
10116 Main St., Ste. 201-B
Bothell, WA 98011
(206) 487-3355
Leadership: P/P
Charge: No

GRAPEVIEW
Kitsap County S.O.S
Martha Lamaack
P.O. Box 82
Grapeview, WA 98546
(206) 275-8076
Leadership: Peer
Charge: No

KENNEWICK
Survivors of Suicide
Richard Nordgren
7525 W. Deschutes Pl.
Kennewick, WA 99336
(509) 783-7416
Leadership: P/P
Charge: No

SEATTLE
Renton/Seattle S.O.S.
Coralie Reed
12044 59th Ave. S.
Seattle, WA 98178
(206) 772-5141
(206) 722-3806, Jean Bowdyes
Leadership: Peer
Charge: No

SILVERDALE
Bremerton Chapter Survivors of
   Suicide

Bremerton Fire Department
Jo-Anne Lott
8835 Sesame NW
Silverdale, WA 98383
Leadership: Peer
Charge: No

SPOKANE
Survivors of a Loved One's Suicide
Lori Hansen
E. 1933 Illinois
Spokane, WA 99207
(509) 838-4428
(509) 483-3310
Leadership: P/P
Charge: No

TACOMA
Pierce County S.O.S. in Tacoma
Lifeline Institute for Suicide Prevention
Marty Hemmann
9307 Bridgeport Way SW
Tacoma, WA 98499
(206) 473-0256
(800) 422-2552
Leadership: Prof
Charge: No

TACOMA
Survivors of Suicide
Marty Himmann
9307 Bridgeport Way SW
Tacoma, WA 98499
(206) 473-0256
(800) 422-2552
Leadership: Peer
Charge: No

TACOMA
Lewis County Survivors Group
Lifeline Institute for Suicide Prevention
Mary Carlson
9307 Bridgeport Way SW
Tacoma, WA 98499
(206) 264-4046
Leadership: Prof
Charge: No

TACOMA
Thurston County Survivors
Group
Lifeline Institute for Suicide Prevention
Gail Hasselholt
9307 Bridgeport Way SW
Tacoma, WA 98499
(206) 438-6887
(200) 422-422-2552
Leadership: Prof
Charge: No

West Virginia

WHEELING
Suicide Survivors Support
Group
Emma C. Wilkins
Box 4043, Warwood Post Office
Wheeling, WV 26003
(304) 277-3916
Leadership: P/P
Charge: No

Wisconsin

APPLETON
Fox Valley S.O.S.

Wichmann Funeral Home
Karen Bork, M.S.E.
537 N. Superior St.
Appleton, WI 54911
(414) 739-1231
Leadership: P/P
Charge: No

EAU CLAIRE
Suicide Survivors Support
  Group
Sacred Heart Hospital/Healing
  Pl
Janet Brick
1010 Oakridge Dr.
Eau Claire, WI 54701
(715) 833-6028
(715) 834-3176
Leadership: Prof
Charge: No

GREEN BAY
Survivors of Suicide
N.E. Wi/Upper Penn Mich
  Group
Don & Jonna Bostedt
630 Greene Ave.
Green Bay, WI 54301
(414) 437-7527
Leadership: P/P
Charge: No

LA CROSSE
Karis Lutheran Hospital/
  La Crosse
Jeanne Kaminski
1910 South Ave.
La Crosse, WI 54601
(608) 785-0530

Leadership: P/P
Charge: No

MADISON
Survivors of Suicide
Emergency Services MHC of
  Dane County
Jeanne Adams
625 W. Washington Ave.
Madison, WI 53703
(608) 251-2345
Leadership: P/P
Charge: No

MARSHFIELD
Study on Suicide
Barb Sisco
604 E. 4th St.
Marshfield, WI 54449
(715) 325-6120
(715) 421-5622
Leadership: Peer
Charge: No

MARSHFIELD
Survivors Helping Survivors
Pastoral Care Department/
  St. Joseph's Hospital
Rev. Dennis W. Olson
611 St. Joseph Ave.
Marshfield, WI 54449
(715) 387-7753
Leadership: Prof
Charge: No

MILWAUKEE
Survivors Helping Survivors
Sewas
Janell Bergholz

734 N. Fourth St., Ste. 325
Milwaukee, WI 53209
(414) 276-3122
Leadership: P/P
Charge: No

SHEBOYGAN
Suicide Loss Support Group
MHA in Sheboygan County
Beverly Randall
2020 Erie Ave.
Sheboygan, WI 53081
(414) 458-3951
(414) 564-3676
Leadership: P/P
Charge: No

Wyoming

CHEYENNE
Share and Care Group

Lynn Conrad
1108 W. 27th St.
Cheyenne, WY 82001
(307) 635-0842
(307) 638-8642, Peggy or Jennifer
Leadership: Peer
Charge: No

New Zealand

CHRISTCHURCH
Canterbury Bereaved by Suicide
  Society
Stephanie Perrott
193 Cashel St., 5th fl.
Christchurch, New Zealand
(*03) 890-825*
(*03) 797-088*, Heather Hapeta
Leadership: P/P
Charge: No

Index

About the Authors

ANN SMOLIN, a certified clinical social worker, is director of the Northern Westchester Branch of Westchester Jewish Community Services, where for five years she has run the longest-established survivor support group in the New York metropolitan area. She completed her undergraduate studies at the University of Wisconsin and at the City College of New York and received her MSW from Yeshiva University. She is a member of the American Association of Suicidology and is in private practice in Westchester County.

JOHN GUINAN is a clinical psychologist who runs a support group for suicide survivors under the auspices of the Wall Street Counseling Center, where he is director. He is also the consulting psychologist for Harbor House, a residential treatment program in the South Bronx, and a therapy supervisor for the Institute for Human Identity in New York. He completed his undergraduate work at the College of the Holy Cross and received his M.A. and Ph.D. in clinical psychology from Fordham University. He maintains a private practice in Croton-on-Hudson.